HAM/THELLO:
THE MOOR OF DENMARK

A new play by William Shakespeare & Jeff Goode

Single copies of plays are sold for reading purposes only. The copying or duplicating of a play, or any part of play, by hand or by any other process, is an infringement of the copyright. Such infringement will be vigorously prosecuted

Baker's Plays
7611 Sunset Blvd.
Los Angeles, CA 90042
BAKERSPLAYS.COM

NOTICE

This book is offered for sale at the price quoted only on the understanding that, if any additional copies of the whole or any part are necessary for its production, such additional copies will be purchased. The attention of all purchasers is directed to the following: This work is protected under the copyright laws of the United States of America, in the British Empire, including the Dominion of Canada, and all other countries adhering to the Universal Copyright Convention. Violations of the Copyright Law are punishable by fine or imprisonment, or both. The copying or duplication of this work or any part of this work, by hand or by any process, is an infringement of the copyright and will be vigorously prosecuted.

This play may not be produced by amateurs or professionals for public or private performance without first submitting application for performing rights. Royalties are due on all performances whether for charity or gain, or whether admission is charged or not. Since performance of this play without the payment of the royalty fee renders anybody participating liable to severe penalties imposed by the law, anybody acting in this play should be sure, before doing so, that the royalty fee has been paid. Professional rights, reading rights, radio broadcasting, television and all mechanical rights, etc. are strictly reserved. Application for performing rights should be made directly to BAKER'S PLAYS.

No one shall commit or authorize any act or omission by which the copyright of, or the right to copyright, this play may be impaired. No one shall make any changes in this play for the purpose of production.

Publication of this play does not imply availability for performance. Both amateurs and professionals considering a production are strongly advised in their own interest to apply to Baker's Plays for written permission before starting rehearsals, advertising, or booking a theatre.

Whenever the play is produced, the author's name must be carried in all publicity, advertising and programs. Also, the following notice must appear on all printed programs, "Produced by special arrangement with Baker's Plays."

Licensing fees for *HAM/THELLO: THE MOOR OF DENMARK*
is based on a per performance rate and payable one week in
advance of the production.
Please consult the Baker's Plays website at www.bakersplays.com or our
current print catalogue for up to date licensing fee information.

Copyright © 2007 by Jeff Goode
Made in U.S.A. All rights reserved.

HAM/THELLO: THE MOOR OF DENMARK
ISBN 978-0-87440-301-5 #1806-B

GENERAL PREFACE TO THE SERIES

They say that "familiarity breeds contempt" and there is no playwright, living or dead, whose work is more familiar to audiences the world over, than William Shakespeare. Four hundred years of almost continuous production, adaptation and recitation have ensured that even the completely uninitiated have a working knowledge of the Bard that can render some of his finest works formulaic.

What grade-schooler doesn't know that the love affair in ROMEO AND JULIET turns out badly? Or that the famous speech in HAMLET goes: "To be, or not to be, yadda yadda yadda..."? And in a medium where suspense is everything—where dramatic twists and comic turns both depend upon the element of surprise—having such a well-versed fan-base can be problematic. Ironically, the most gifted dramatist in history is often hard-pressed to impress our jaded modern audience, simply because it is impossible to remove their foreknowledge of the story and allow them to experience the plays in the unadulterated context in which Shakespeare's contemporaries saw them for the very first time.

The New Plays of William Shakespeare were developed as a means to a fresh perspective on these classic texts. Each play in the series intertwines two of the extant works to create an original script with authentically Shakespearean language, verse and characters, in new and unexpected situations whose outcome may still be in doubt.

The plays in this series are designed to be read, performed and enjoyed just as you would the traditional works of Shakespeare. Performers familiar with the canon will find that great lengths have been taken to preserve the integrity and intention of the original verse, rhyme and imagery. Conventions of Elizabethan stagecraft, dramaturgical analysis and scansion apply to the new plays as to the originals. Only the action is up in the air.

The series also seeks to address challenges common to present day production companies, such as cast size and imbalance of male and female roles.

It is hoped that these plays might offer both performers and audiences new insight into the genius and mastery of Shakespeare, freed of a few centuries' preconception, and perhaps with a few surprises still intact.

HAM/THELLO: THE MOOR OF DENMARK was first performed September 1st, 2007, at the John F. Kennedy Center for the Performing Arts in Washington, as part of the Page-to-Stage New Play Festival, a production of the Washington Shakespeare Company.

Directed by Gaurav Gopalan

Featuring:

Robert Rector
as Hamlet

Theo Hadjimichael
as Othello

Leslie Sarah Cohen
as Ophelia

Suejin Song
as Desdemona

elisha efua bartels
as Iago

Jessica Lynn Roderiguez
as Bianca and Player Queen

Frank Britton
as Player King and Clown

Melissa Hmelnicky
as Horatio

John Geoffrion

J.J. Area

William LeDent

Directorial Assistant
Lewis Stevenson

THE MOOR'S DENMARK

It is a time of war in peace-loving Denmark, and only the heroics of their Moorish general Othello have saved the pacifist Danes from the invading Poles.

With the sudden and unexpected death of the late King Hamlet, the Danes (and Queen Desdemona) have rewarded their victorious general with the crown of Denmark, to the consternation of those loyal to the old King and young Prince Hamlet.

DRAMATIS PERSONAE

OTHELLO, *King of Denmark, a noble Moor in military service to the Danes*
HAMLET, *son to the late King*
IAGO, *Othello's jester*
HORATIO, *friend to Hamlet*
MARCELLUS, *a soldier*

DESDEMONA, *Queen of Denmark, mother to Hamlet*
OPHELIA, *daughter to Iago, bodyguard to the Queen*
BIANCA, *a henchperson*

FRANCISCO, *a soldier*
PLAYERS
CLOWN, *servant to Ophelia*

Lords, Ladies, Officers, Soldiers, Herald, Gentlemen and Attendants

DOUBLING OF ROLES

In Elizabethan and Jacobean England, it was illegal for women to appear upon the public stage. Hence, the plays of Shakespeare were written to be performed by an all-male company of actors with only a handful of female characters – largely secondary roles played by boys.

These male-heavy casts present a challenge in modern-day stagings, where acting companies usually consist of a more balanced troupe of men and women. To accommodate this, gender-blind casting[1] is recommended for the plays of Shakespeare, as well as gender-reversal[2], to adapt the plays to the available talent pool.

For example, the following breakdown for this play yields an abbreviated cast of nine actors - five men, four women:

MALE	FEMALE
Othello	Desdemona
Hamlet	Ophelia
Iago	Bianca / Attendant / Clown
Horatio	Francisco / Herald / Player
Marcellus / Player	

---

[1] Casting the best actor for the part, regardless of their gender.
[2] Changing the sex of the character to fit the actor who will be playing the part.

ABOUT THE AUTHORS

William Shakespeare is an English poet and playwright, generally regarded as the greatest writer in the English language, and by many as the greatest dramatist in history. His extant work includes 37 plays, 154 sonnets, and a number of other poems and collaborations. His plays have been translated into virtually every language and performed throughout the world.

Jeff Goode is an American director, playwright and screenwriter. He is the creator of the Disney Channel's animated series *American Dragon: Jake Long*, and the author of over 50 plays and musicals, including *The Eight: Reindeer Monologues*.

NEW PLAYS BY WILLIAM SHAKESPEARE & JEFF GOODE:
Romeo & Julius [Caesar]
Ham/thello: the Moor of Denmark
Lear's Labour's Lost

ACT I – The Ghost on the Platform

SCENE 1 – Elsinore. A platform before the castle.

   *(**FRANCISCO**, a sentinel, at his post. Enter **IAGO** the king's jester.)*

IAGO. Who's there?

FRANCISCO. Nay, answer me: stand, and unfold yourself.

IAGO. Long live the king!

FRANCISCO. Iago?

IAGO. He.

FRANCISCO. You come most carefully upon your hour.

IAGO. 'Tis now struck twelve; get thee to bed, Francisco.
   If you do meet Horatio and Marcellus,
   The rivals of my watch, bid them make haste.

FRANCISCO. Long live the king!

IAGO.   Long live good King Othello.

   *(Exit **FRANCISCO**. Enter **BIANCA**, with a **GHOST** costume.)*

BIANCA. Thou told'st me thou didst hold him in thy hate.

   *(**IAGO** helps **BIANCA** into her disguise.)*

IAGO. I have told thee often, and I re-tell thee again and again, I hate the Moor:
   Despise me, if I do not. Three great ones of the city,
   In personal suit to make me his lieutenant,
   Off-capp'd to him: and, by the faith of man,
   I know my price, I am worth no worse a place:
   But he; as loving his own pride and purposes,
   Nonsuits my mediators; for, 'Certes,' says he,
   'I have already chose my officer.'

And what was he? Forsooth, a great politician,
   Prince Hamlet, son of King Othello's queen.
   He, in good time, must his lieutenant be,
   And I—God bless the mark!—his Moorship's jester.

BIANCA. By heaven, I rather would have been his hangman.

IAGO. Why, there's no remedy; 'tis the curse of service,
   Preferment goes by letter and affection,
   And not by old gradation, where each second
   Stood heir to the first. So now, be judge yourself,
   Whether I in any just term am affined
   To love the Moor.

BIANCA. I would not follow him then.

IAGO.   O, sooth, content you;
   I follow him to serve my turn upon him:
   Heaven is my judge, not I for love and duty,
   But seeming so, for my peculiar end.

BIANCA. What a fall fortune does the thicklips owe
   If he can carry't thus!

IAGO. My cause is hearted; thine hath no less reason. Let us be conjunctive in our revenge against him.

BIANCA. I think I hear them.

IAGO.   You were best go in.
   Thou art sure of me:—go, make mischief.

   (*Exit* **BIANCA**.)

   Alas, poor rogue! I think, i' faith, she loves me.
   While I mine own gain'd knowledge should profane,
   If I would time expend with such a snipe.
   But for my sport and profit.

   (*Enter* **HORATIO** *and* **MARCELLUS**.)

   Stand, ho! Who's there?

HORATIO. Friends to this ground.

MARCELLUS.   And liegemen to the Moor.

IAGO. What, is Horatio there?
HORATIO. A piece of him.
IAGO. Welcome, Horatio: welcome, good Marcellus.
MARCELLUS. What, has this thing appear'd again to-night?
IAGO. I have seen nothing.
MARCELLUS. Horatio says 'tis but our fantasy,
And will not let belief take hold of him
Touching this dreaded sight, twice seen of us.
HORATIO. Tush, tush, 'twill not appear.
IAGO. Sit down awhile;
And let us once again assail your ears,
That are so fortified against our story
What we have two nights seen—

(Enter **BIANCA**, *disguised as a* **GHOST**.*)*

MARCELLUS. Peace, break thee off; look, where it comes again!
IAGO. In the same figure, like the king that's dead.
MARCELLUS. Thou art a scholar; speak to it, Horatio.
IAGO. Looks it not like the king? mark it, Horatio.
HORATIO. Most like: it harrows me with fear and wonder.
IAGO. It would be spoke to.
MARCELLUS. Question it, Horatio.
HORATIO. What art thou that usurp'st this time of night,
Together with that fair and warlike form
In which the majesty of buried Denmark
Did sometimes march? by heaven I charge thee, speak!
IAGO. It is offended.
MARCELLUS. See, it stalks away!
HORATIO. Stay! speak, speak! I charge thee, speak!

(Exit **GHOST**.*)*

IAGO. How now, Horatio! you tremble and look pale:
Is not this something more than fantasy?

HORATIO. Before my God, I might not this believe
Without the sensible and true avouch
Of mine own eyes.

IAGO. Is it not like the king?

HORATIO. As thou art to thyself.

MARCELLUS. Thus twice before, and jump at this dead hour,
With martial stalk hath he gone by our watch.

HORATIO. In what particular thought to work I know not;
But in the gross and scope of my opinion,
This bodes some strange eruption to our state.

MARCELLUS. A mote it is to trouble the mind's eye.

IAGO. But soft, behold! lo, where it comes again!

(Re-enter **GHOST**.*)*

HORATIO. I'll cross it, though it blast me. Stay, illusion!

(Cock crows.)

If thou art privy to thy country's fate,
Which, happily, foreknowing may avoid, O, speak!
Speak of it: stay, and speak! Stop it, Marcellus.

MARCELLUS. Shall I strike at it with my partisan?

HORATIO. Do, if it will not stand.

IAGO. 'Tis here!

HORATIO. 'Tis here!

MARCELLUS. 'Tis gone!

(Exit **GHOST**.*)*

IAGO. It was about to speak, when the cock crew.

MARCELLUS. Let us impart what we have seen to-night
Unto young Hamlet; for, upon my life,
This spirit, dumb to us, will speak to him.

HORATIO. Let's do't, I pray; and I this morning know
Where we shall find him most conveniently.

IAGO. Pray you, lead on.

(Exeunt.)

SCENE 2 – *A street.*

(Enter a **HERALD** *with a proclamation.)*

HERALD. It is King Othello's pleasure, our noble and valiant general, that, upon certain tidings now arrived, importing the mere perdition of the Polish fleet, every man put himself into triumph; some to dance, some to make bonfires, each man to what sport and revels his addiction leads him: for, besides these beneficial news, it is the celebration of his nuptial. So much was his pleasure should be proclaimed. All offices are open, and there is full liberty of feasting from this present hour of five till the bell have told eleven. Heaven bless the state of Denmark and his royal majesty Othello!

(Exit.)

SCENE 3 – *A room of state in the castle.*

> (*Enter* **KING OTHELLO**, **QUEEN DESDEMONA**, **OPHELIA** *the queen's bodyguard, Lords, and Attendants, and* **PRINCE HAMLET**, *drunk.*)

OTHELLO. Though yet of Hamlet our dear sovereign's death
The memory be green, and that it us befitted
To bear our hearts in grief and our whole kingdom
To be contracted in one brow of woe,
Yet so far hath discretion fought with nature
That we with wisest sorrow think on him,
Together with remembrance of ourselves.
Therefore our sometime queen, and now our wife,
Have we, as 'twere with a defeated joy,—
With mirth in funeral and with dirge in marriage,
Taken to wife: nor have we herein barr'd
Your better wisdoms, which have freely gone
With this affair along. For all, our thanks.
But now, lieutenant Hamlet, and my son,—

HAMLET. *[Aside]* A little more than kin, and less than kind.

OTHELLO. How is it that the clouds still hang on you?

HAMLET. Not so, my lord; I am too much i' the sun.

DESDEMONA. Good Hamlet, cast thy nighted colour off,
And let thine eye look like a friend on Denmark.

OTHELLO. 'Tis sweet and commendable in your nature, Hamlet,
To give these mourning duties to your father:
But now, good son, we pray you, throw to earth
This unprevailing woe, and think of us
As of a father: for let the world take note,
You are the most immediate to our throne;
And with no less nobility of love
Than that which dearest father bears his son,
Do I impart toward you. For your intent
In going back to school in Wittenberg,

It is most retrograde to our desire:
And we beseech you, bend you to remain
Here, in the cheer and comfort of our eye,
Our chiefest courtier, captain, and our son.

DESDEMONA. Let not thy mother lose her prayers, Hamlet:
I pray thee, stay with us; go not to Wittenberg.

HAMLET. *[To* **OTHELLO***]* O thou foul thief, where hast thou stow'd my mother?
Damn'd as thou art, thou hast enchanted her;
For I'll refer me to all things of sense,
If she in chains of magic were not bound,
Whether a queen so loyal, fair and happy,
Would ever have, to incur a general mock,
Run from her grievage to the sooty bosom
Of such a thing as thou, to fear, not to delight.
It is a judgment maim'd and most imperfect
Why this should be. I therefore vouch again
That with some mixtures powerful o'er the blood,
Or with some dram conjured to this effect,
Thou wrought upon her.

OTHELLO. To vouch this, is no proof.

DESDEMONA. Come, hold your peace.

HAMLET. 'Twill out, 'twill out: I peace?
No, I will speak as liberal as the north:
Let heaven and men and devils, let them all,
All, all, cry shame against me, yet I'll speak.

(Points to a portrait of the late King hanging over the throne.)

This was your husband. Look you now, what follows:
Here is your husband; like a mildew'd ear,
Blasting his wholesome brother. Have you eyes?
Could you on this fair mountain leave to feed,
And batten on this moor? Ha! have you eyes?
So excellent a king; that was, to this,

Hyperion to a satyr;—

DESDEMONA. Come, you're drunk.

HAMLET. A king of shreds and patches,— Drunk!

OTHELLO. Be wise,
And get you home.

HAMLET. I will not. Let me go, sir,
Or I'll knock you o'er the mazzard.

OTHELLO. I'll make thee an example.

HAMLET. Do thy worst.

(**OTHELLO** *threatens to strike* **HAMLET**. **DESDEMONA**
comes between them.)

DESDEMONA. Nay, good Othello;
I pray you, sweet, hold your hand.
[To **HAMLET***]* For Christian shame, put by this barbarous brawl.

OTHELLO. Hamlet, I love thee,
But never more be officer of mine.
[To **DESDEMONA***]* Come, my dear love,
The purchase made, the fruits are to ensue;
That profit's yet to come 'tween me and you.
Good night.

DESDEMONA. We will have more of this to-morrow.
Hamlet, good night: to-morrow with your earliest
Let me have speech with you.

HAMLET. I shall in all my best obey you, madam.

OTHELLO. Go, Hamlet, look you to the guard to-night.
[To **DESDEMONA***]* Come away.

(*Exeunt all but* **HAMLET**.)

HAMLET. O, that this too too solid flesh would melt
Thaw and resolve itself into a dew!
Or that the Everlasting had not fix'd
His canon 'gainst self-slaughter! O God! God!
How weary, stale, flat and unprofitable,

Seem to me all the uses of this world!
But break, my heart; for I must hold my tongue.

(Exit **HAMLET**. *Re-enter* **OPHELIA** *and Attendant.)*

ATTENDANT. O thou invisible spirit of wine, if thou hast no name to be known by, let us call thee devil!

OPHELIA. But is he often thus?

ATTENDANT. 'Tis evermore the prologue to his sleep:
He'll watch the horologe a double set,
If drink rock not his cradle.

OPHELIA. O God, that men should put an enemy in their mouths to steal away their brains!

ATTENDANT. O heavenly powers, restore him!

(Enter **IAGO**. *Attendant exits.)*

IAGO. What is't, Ophelia, she hath said to you?

OPHELIA. So please you, something touching the Lord Hamlet.

IAGO. Marry, well bethought:
'Tis told me, he hath very oft of late
Given private time to you; and you yourself
Have of your audience been most free and bounteous:
If it be so, as so 'tis put on me,
And that in way of caution, I must tell you,
I would not, in plain terms, from this time forth,
Have you so slander any moment leisure,
As to give words or talk with the Lord Hamlet.
Look to't, I charge you: come your ways.

OPHELIA. But, good my father,
He hath given countenance to his speech, my lord,
With almost all the holy vows of heaven.

IAGO. Ay, springes to catch woodcocks. I do know,
When the blood burns, how prodigal the soul
Lends the tongue vows: these blazes, daughter,
You must not take for fire. From this time
Be somewhat scanter of your maiden presence,

Else weigh what loss your honour may sustain,
If with too credent ear you list his songs,
Or lose your heart, or your chaste treasure open
To his unmaster'd importunity.
Fear it, Ophelia, fear it, my dear daughter,
And keep you in the rear of your affection,
Out of the shot and danger of desire.

OPHELIA. I shall the effect of this good lesson keep,
As watchman to my heart.

IAGO. For Hamlet and the trifling of his favour,
Hold it a fashion and a toy in blood;
No more.

OPHELIA. No more but so?

IAGO. Think it no more.

OPHELIA. I shall obey, my lord.

(Exeunt.)

SCENE 4 – *The lobby of the castle.*

(Enter **HAMLET**. *Enter to him,* **HORATIO** *and* **MARCELLUS**.*)*

HORATIO. Hail to your lordship!
HAMLET. I am glad to see you well:
Horatio,—or I do forget myself.
HORATIO. The same, my lord, and your poor servant ever.
HAMLET. But what, in faith, make you from Wittenberg?
We'll teach you to drink deep ere you depart.
HORATIO. My lord, I came to see your father's funeral.
HAMLET. I pray thee, do not mock me, fellow-student;
I think it was to see my mother's wedding.
HORATIO. Indeed, my lord, it follow'd hard upon.
HAMLET. Thrift, thrift, Horatio! the funeral baked meats
Did coldly furnish forth the marriage tables.
Would I had met my dearest foe in heaven
Or ever I had seen that day, Horatio!
My father!—methinks I see my father.
HORATIO. Where, my lord?
HAMLET. In my mind's eye, Horatio.
HORATIO. My lord, I think I saw him yesternight.
HAMLET. Saw? who?
HORATIO. My lord, the king your father.
HAMLET. The king my father?
HORATIO. Two nights together had this gentlemen,
Marcellus, and Iago, on their watch,
In the dead vast and middle of the night,
Been thus encounter'd. A figure like your father
Appears before them, and with solemn march
Goes slow and stately by them: thrice he walk'd
By their oppress'd and fear-surprisèd eyes.
And I with them the third night kept the watch.

HAMLET. But where was this?

MARCELLUS. My lord, upon the platform where we watch'd.

HAMLET. I would I had been there.

HORATIO. It would have much amazed you.

HAMLET. I will watch to-night;
   Perchance 'twill walk again.

HORATIO.   I warrant it will.

HAMLET. Upon the platform, 'twixt eleven and twelve,
   I'll visit you.

HORATIO & MARCELLUS. Our duty to your honour.

HAMLET. Your loves, as mine to you: farewell.

   (Exeunt all but **HAMLET.***)*

   Till then sit still, my soul: foul deeds will rise,
   Though all the earth o'erwhelm them, to men's eyes.

   (Enter **IAGO**, *with drink.)*

   Welcome, Iago; we must to the watch.

IAGO. Not this hour, lieutenant; 'tis not yet ten o' the clock. Our general cast us thus early for the love of his Desdemona; who let us not therefore blame: he hath not yet made wanton the night with her; and she is sport for Jove.

HAMLET. Let me not think on't—Frailty, thy name is woman!—

IAGO. Well, happiness to their sheets!— Come, lieutenant, I have a stoup of wine; and here without are a brace of Danish gallants that would fain have a measure to the health of black Othello.

HAMLET. Not to-night, good Iago: I have very poor and unhappy brains for drinking: I could well wish courtesy would invent some other custom of entertainment.

IAGO. O, they are our friends; but one cup: I'll drink for you.

HAMLET. I have drunk but one cup to-night, and dare not task my weakness with any more.

IAGO. What, man! 'tis a night of revels: the gallants desire it.

HAMLET. Where are they?

IAGO. Here at the door; I pray you, call them in.

HAMLET. I'll do't; but it dislikes me.

(Exit.)

IAGO. If I can fasten but one cup upon him,
With that which he hath drunk to-night already,
The better shall my purpose work on him.
Some wine, ho!

*(Exit, and re-enter with **HAMLET** and others, singing.)*

And let me the canakin clink, clink;
And let me the canakin clink
A soldier's a man;
A life's but a span;
Why, then, let a soldier drink.
Some wine, boys!

HAMLET. 'Fore God, an excellent song.

IAGO. To the health of our general!

HAMLET. To the platform, masters; come, let's set the watch.

(IAGO *follows him out, singing.)*

IAGO. *King Stephen was a worthy peer,*
His breeches cost him but a crown;
He held them sixpence all too dear,
With that he call'd the tailor lown—

(Exeunt.)

SCENE 5 – *The platform.*

(Enter **HORATIO** *and* **MARCELLUS**.*)*

MARCELLUS. The air bites shrewdly; it is very cold.

HORATIO. It is a nipping and an eager air.

HAMLET. What hour now?

HORATIO.   I think it lacks of twelve.

MARCELLUS. No, it is struck.

HORATIO. Indeed? I heard it not: then it draws near the season

Wherein the spirit held his wont to walk.

(Enter **HAMLET** *and* **IAGO**, *singing.)*

IAGO & HAMLET. *He was a wight of high renown,*
And thou art but of low degree:
'Tis pride that pulls the country down;
Then take thine auld cloak about thee.

HAMLET. Why, this is a more exquisite song than the other.

IAGO. Some wine, ho!

HAMLET. Do not think, gentlemen. I am drunk: this is my ancient; this is my right hand, and this is my left: I am not drunk now; I can stand well enough, and speak well enough.

ALL. Excellent well.

HAMLET. Why, very well then; you must not think then that I am drunk.

HORATIO & MARCELLUS. My lord, we will not.

IAGO. Call up your father,
Rouse him: make after him, poison his delight.
What, ho, King Hamlet!

HAMLET.   Father, Hamlet, ho!

IAGO. Awake! what, ho, King Hamlet! thieves! thieves! thieves!
Look to your crown, your kingdom and your wife!
Thieves! thieves!

HAMLET. Even now, now, very now, an old black ram
   Is topping your white ewe. Arise, arise;
   Or else the devil will make a cuckold of you.

IAGO. Arise, I say.
   You'll have your Desdemona covered with a Barbary
   horse; you'll have your half-sons neigh to you; you'll
   have coursers for cousins and gennets for germans.

HORATIO. Look, my lord, it comes!

   (Enter **BIANCA**, *disguised as the* **GHOST**.*)*

GHOST. What is the reason of this terrible summons?
   What is the matter there?

   *(***HAMLET** *is stricken sober.)*

HAMLET. Angels and ministers of grace defend us!

IAGO. Why, but you are now well enough: how came you
   thus recovered?

HAMLET. It hath pleased the devil drunkenness to give
   place to the devil dread; one unperfectness shows me
   another, to make me frankly despise myself.

   *(***GHOST** *beckons* **HAMLET**.*)*

MARCELLUS. It beckons you to go away with it,
   As if it some impartment did desire
   To you alone.

HAMLET.   Then I will follow it.

HORATIO. What if it tempt you toward the flood, my lord,
   Or to the dreadful summit of the cliff
   That beetles o'er his base into the sea.

MARCELLUS. You shall not go, my lord.

HAMLET.   Hold off your
   hands.

HORATIO. Be ruled; you shall not go.

HAMLET.   My fate cries out,
   Still am I call'd. Unhand me, gentlemen.
   By heaven, I'll make a ghost of him that lets me!
   I say, away! Go on; I'll follow thee.

(Exeunt **GHOST** *and* **HAMLET**.*)*

MARCELLUS. Something is rotten in the state of Denmark.
HORATIO. Heaven will direct it.
MARCELLUS. Nay, let's follow him.

(Exeunt.)

SCENE 6 – *Another part of the platform.*

(Enter **GHOST** *and* **HAMLET**.*)*

HAMLET. Where wilt thou lead me? speak; I'll go no further.

GHOST. Mark me.

HAMLET. I will. Speak; I am bound to hear.

GHOST. So art thou to revenge, when thou shalt hear.

HAMLET. What?

GHOST. I am thy father's spirit,
Doom'd for a certain term to walk the night,
Till the foul crimes done in my days of nature
Are burnt and purged away. But that I am forbid
To tell the secrets of my prison-house,
I could a tale unfold whose lightest word
Would harrow up thy soul. List, list, O, list!
If thou didst ever thy dear father love—

HAMLET. O God!

GHOST. Revenge his foul and most unnatural murder.

HAMLET. Murder!

GHOST. Murder most foul, as in the best it is;
But this most foul, strange and unnatural.

HAMLET. Haste me to know't, that I, with wings as swift,
May sweep to my revenge.

GHOST. I find thee apt;
'Tis given out that, sleeping in my orchard,
A serpent stung me; so the whole ear of Denmark
Is by a forgèd process of my death
Rankly abused: but know, thou noble youth,
The serpent that did sting thy father's life
Now wears his crown.

HAMLET. O my prophetic soul!
Othello!

GHOST. But, soft! methinks I scent the morning air;

Brief let me be. Sleeping within my orchard,
My custom always of the afternoon,
Upon my secure hour Othello stole,
With juice of cursèd hebenon in a vial,
And in the porches of my ears did pour't.
Thus was I, sleeping, by Othello's hand
Of life, of crown, of queen, at once dispatch'd:
If thou hast nature in thee, bear it not.

HAMLET. My black and bloody thoughts, with violent pace,
Shall ne'er look back, ne'er ebb to humble love,
Till that a capable and wide revenge
Swallow him up. Now, by yond marble heaven,
In the due reverence of a sacred vow
I here engage my words.

GHOST. Adieu, adieu! Hamlet, remember me.

(Exit.)

HAMLET. Ay, thou poor ghost, while memory holds a seat
In this distracted globe. Remember thee!
O most pernicious woman!
O villain, villain, smiling, damnèd villain!

HORATIO & MARCELLUS.
[Within] My lord, my lord,—

(Enter **HORATIO**, **MARCELLUS** *and* **IAGO**.*)*

MARCELLUS. Lord Hamlet,—
HORATIO. Heaven secure him!
HAMLET. Hillo, ho, ho, boy! come, bird, come.
MARCELLUS. How is't, my noble lord?
HORATIO. What news, my lord?
HAMLET. O, wonderful!
IAGO. Good my lord, tell it.
HAMLET. No; you'll reveal it.
HORATIO. Not I, my lord, by heaven.
MARCELLUS. Nor I, my lord.

HAMLET. Come hither, gentlemen,
   And lay your hands upon my sword, and swear:
   Never to speak of this that you have heard,
   Swear by my sword.
GHOST. *[Beneath]* Swear.
HAMLET. Never make known what you have seen to-night.
HORATIO, MARCELLUS & IAGO. My lord, we will not.
GHOST. *[Beneath]* Swear.
HAMLET. Rest, rest, perturbèd spirit!

   (They swear.)

   Let us go in together;
   And still your fingers on your lips, I pray.

   (Exit **HORATIO** *and* **MARCELLUS.** *)*

   The time is out of joint: O cursèd spite,
   That ever I was born to set it right!
IAGO. What's the matter, lieutenant?
HAMLET. Iago,—
IAGO. What say'st thou, noble heart?
HAMLET. What will I do, thinkest thou?
IAGO. Why, go to bed, and sleep.
HAMLET. I will incontinently drown myself.
IAGO. If thou dost, I shall never love thee after.
   Why, thou silly gentleman!
HAMLET. It is silliness to live when to live is torment; and then have we a prescription to die when death is our physician.
IAGO. O villainous! If thou wilt needs damn thyself, do it a more delicate way than drowning. Come, be a man. Drown thyself! drown cats and blind puppies.
HAMLET. I do not know
   Why yet I live to say 'This thing's to do;'
   Sith I have cause and will and not the means
   To do't. The general will not speak with me.
IAGO. What, man! there are ways to recover the general again.

HAMLET. I will ask him for my place again; he shall tell me I am a drunkard!

IAGO. You or any man living may be drunk! at a time, man. I'll tell you what you shall do. Our general's wife is now the general: confess yourself freely to her; importune her help to put you in your place again: this broken joint between you and her husband entreat her to splinter; and, my fortunes against any lay worth naming, this crack of your love shall grow stronger than it was before.

HAMLET. Then is doomsday near.

IAGO. Wear thy good rapier bare, and put it home.

HAMLET. Indeed, la, without an oath, I'll make an end on't.

IAGO. Cudgel thy brains no more about it.

HAMLET. You advise me well. And betimes in the morning I will beseech the virtuous Desdemona to undertake for me: I am desperate of my fortunes if they cheque me here.

IAGO. Ply Desdemona well, and you are sure on't.

(*Exit* **HAMLET**.)

And what's he then that says I play the villain?
When this advice is free I give and honest,
Probal to thinking and indeed the course
To win the Moor again?
How am I then a villain
To counsel Hamlet to this parallel course,
Directly to his good? Divinity of hell!
When devils will the blackest sins put on,
They do suggest at first with heavenly shows,
As I do now: for whiles this honest fool
Plies Desdemona to repair his fortunes
And she for him pleads strongly to the Moor,
I'll pour this pestilence into his ear:
That he is too familiar with his wife.

After some time, to abuse Othello's ear
That she repeals him for her body's lust;
And by how much she strives to do him good,
She shall undo her credit with the Moor.
So will I turn her virtue into pitch,
And out of her own goodness make the net
That shall enmesh them all.

(Exit.)

ACT II – The Handkerchief

SCENE 1 – A street. Beneath Ophelia's window.

(*Enter* **HAMLET**.)

HAMLET. Hillo, ho, ho, my sweet! I do beseech you
That I may speak with you! How now, Ophelia!

(*Enter* **CLOWN** [*Ophelia's Attendant*].)

CLOWN. How, sir, how! What, have you lost your wits?
HAMLET. Dost thou hear, my honest friend?
CLOWN. No, I hear not your honest friend; I hear you.
HAMLET. Prithee, keep up thy quillets. There's a poor piece of gold for thee: if the gentlewoman that attends the general's wife be stirring, tell her there's one Hamlet entreats her a little favour of speech: wilt thou do this?
CLOWN. She is stirring, sir: if she will stir hither, I shall seem to notify unto her.
HAMLET. Do, good my friend.
CLOWN. Before me! look, where she comes.

(*Enter* **OPHELIA**, *armed*.)

OPHELIA. What, are you mad? I charge you, get you home.
HAMLET. Hail to thee, lady! and the grace of heaven,
Before, behind thee, and on every hand,
Enwheel thee all around!
OPHELIA.   The worser welcome:
I have charged thee not to haunt about my doors:
In honest plainness thou hast heard me say
That I am not for thee; and now, in madness,
Being full of supper and distempering draughts,

Upon malicious bravery, dost thou come
To start my quiet.

HAMLET. Patience, good maid.—

OPHELIA. But thou must needs be sure
My spirit and my place have in them power
To make this bitter to thee.

(She draws her rapier.)

HAMLET. Diablo, ho!
God's will, Ophelia, hold!

*(**HAMLET** offers her a pair of letters.)*

Here's letters seal'd:
This to her majesty; this to yourself.
Yet, I beseech you,— Dost thou hear, Ophelia?
If you think fit, or that it may be done,
Give me advantage of some brief discourse
With Desdemona alone.

*(**OPHELIA** seizes the letters and thrashes him with them.)*

OPHELIA. Nay, get thee gone.
By the mass, 'tis morning;
Retire thee; go where thou art billeted:
Away, I say! My house is not a grange.
*[to **CLOWN**]* Come, guard the door without; let him not pass.

*(Exit **OPHELIA** and **CLOWN**. Enter **IAGO**.)*

HAMLET. In happy time, Iago.

IAGO. You have not been a-bed, then?

HAMLET. Why, no; the day had broke
Before we parted.

IAGO. What is the matter, my lord?

HAMLET. I have made bold, Iago,
To send in to your daughter: my suit to her
Is, that she will to virtuous Desdemona

Procure me some access.
There is no other way; 'tis she must do't.

IAGO. Do you withdraw yourself a little while,
I'll send her to you presently.

HAMLET. I humbly thank you for't.

(Exit **HAMLET.***)*

IAGO. Two things are to be done:
My daughter must for Hamlet move her mistress;
I'll set her on;
Myself the while to draw the Moor apart,
And bring him jump when he may Hamlet find
Soliciting his wife: ay, that's the way
Dull not device by coldness and delay.
[Calls within] How now, Ophelia! what's the matter?

(Re-enter **OPHELIA.***)*

OPHELIA. O, my lord, my lord, I have been so affrighted!

IAGO. With what, i' the name of God?

OPHELIA. My lord, as I was studying my rapier
Lord Hamlet, with his doublet all unbraced;
As if he had been loosèd out of hell
To speak of horrors,—he comes before me.

IAGO. Mad for thy love?

OPHELIA. My lord, I do not know;
But truly, I do fear it.

(Gives him the letters.)

Here is a letter;
And here another: the one of them imports
His noble love in honourable fashion.

IAGO. Ay, fashion you may call it; go to, go to.
What, have you given him any hard words of late?

OPHELIA. No, my good lord, but, as you did command,
I did repel his fetters and denied
His access to me.

IAGO. That hath made him mad.
Come, go with me: I will go seek the king.
This must be known; which, being kept close, might move
More grief to hide than hate to utter love.
Fetch Desdemona hither. The affair cries haste,
And speed must answer it.
Bid her come hither: go.

OPHELIA. I will, my lord.

(Exit OPHELIA. IAGO reads over the letters.)

IAGO. Words, words, words.
This is too long.
It shall to the barber's.

(Tears the letter in half.)

Now here's another discontented paper:
I'll tear it all to pieces.

(Tears the second letter to pieces.)

I confess it is my shame to be so rash; but it is in my virtue to amend it;

(Pieces the letter back together again, in a different order.)

Devise a new commission, write it fair:

(The task completed, IAGO admires his creation.)

O, 'tis most sweet,
When in one line two crafts directly meet.
And this may help to thicken other proofs
That do demonstrate thinly.

(Exit.)

SCENE 2 – *The lobby of the castle.*

(Enter **KING OTHELLO**, **HORATIO**, **MARCELLUS**, *and Attendants.)*

OTHELLO. Welcome, Marcellus and my dear Horatio!
The need we have to use you did provoke
Our hasty sending. Something have you heard
Of Hamlet's transformation; so call it,
Sith nor the exterior nor the inward man
Resembles that it was. What it should be,
More than his father's death, that thus hath put him
So much from the understanding of himself,
I cannot dream of: I entreat you both,
That, being of so young days brought up with him,
That you vouchsafe your rest here in our court
Some little time: so by your companies
To draw him on to pleasures, and to gather
Whether aught, to us unknown, afflicts him thus,
That, open'd, lies within our remedy.

(Enter **IAGO**.*)*

HORATIO. Your majesty might, by your sovereign power,
Put your dread pleasures more into command
Than to entreaty.

MARCELLUS. But we both obey.

OTHELLO. Thanks, good Marcellus and Horatio.

(Exit **MARCELLUS** *and* **HORATIO**.*)*

IAGO. This business is well ended.
And I do think, my lord, that I have found
The head and source of all your son's distemper.

OTHELLO. O, speak of that; that do I long to hear.

IAGO. I will be brief: your noble son is mad.

OTHELLO. Mad call you it?
He is importunate, indeed distract.—

IAGO. That he is mad, 'tis true: 'tis true 'tis pity;

And pity 'tis 'tis true: a foolish figure.
I have a daughter—have while she is mine—
Who, in her duty and obedience, mark,
Hath given me this:

(Shows **OTHELLO** *the letter.)*

Know you the hand?

OTHELLO. 'Tis Hamlet's character.

IAGO. Letters, my lord, from Hamlet:
Found in the pocket of Queen Desdemona.

OTHELLO. Ha!

IAGO. Now gather, and surmise.
[Reads] 'To the celestial and my soul's idol, the most beautified— Desdemona,— In her excellent white bosom, these, &c.'—

OTHELLO. Came this from Hamlet to her?

IAGO. Good general, stay awhile; I will be faithful.
[Reads] 'Doubt thou the stars are fire;
Doubt that the sun doth move;
Doubt truth to be a liar;
But never doubt I love.—

'O Desdemona,— You shall know I am set naked on your kingdom— I have not art to reckon my groans: but that I love thee best, O most best, believe it. Adieu.— Thine evermore, most dear lady, whilst this machine is to him, HAMLET.'

OTHELLO. How! is this true?

IAGO. Here's the commission: read it at more leisure.

*(***OTHELLO** *takes the letter from* **IAGO***, and reads it over.)*

OTHELLO. 'Naked'! And in a postscript here, he says 'alone.'

IAGO. This, in obedience, hath my daughter shown me,
And more above, hath his solicitings,
As they fell out by time, by means and place,
All given to mine ear.—

OTHELLO. What means this, my lord?

IAGO. But how hath she
Received his love?

OTHELLO. What dost thou say, Iago?

IAGO. I must tell thee this—Desdemona is directly in love with him.

OTHELLO. With him! why, 'tis not possible.

IAGO. You have seen nothing then?

OTHELLO. Nor ever heard, nor ever did suspect.

IAGO. Yes, you have seen Hamlet and she together.

OTHELLO. But then I saw no harm, and then I heard
Each syllable that breath made up between them.

IAGO. What, did they never whisper?

OTHELLO. Never, my lord.

IAGO. Nor send you out o' the way?

OTHELLO. Never.

IAGO. To fetch her fan, her gloves, her mask, nor nothing?

OTHELLO. Never, my lord.

IAGO. Nay, but be wise: yet we see nothing done.

OTHELLO. I do not think but Desdemona's honest.

IAGO. Long live she so! and long live you to think so!

OTHELLO. Think so, Iago!

IAGO. I dare be sworn I think that she is honest.

OTHELLO. Think, my lord?

IAGO. I do not know, my lord, what I should think.

OTHELLO. Give me a living reason she's disloyal.

IAGO. What,
If I had said I had seen him do you wrong?
Or heard him say,—

OTHELLO. Hath he said any thing?

IAGO. I think nothing, my lord.

OTHELLO. Come, deal justly with me: come, come; nay, speak.
Be even and direct with me.

IAGO. I do not like the office:
    But, sith I am enter'd in this cause so far,
    Prick'd to't by foolish honesty and love,
    I will go on. I lay with Hamlet lately;
    And, being troubled with a raging tooth,
    I could not sleep.
    There are a kind of men so loose of soul,
    That in their sleeps will mutter their affairs:
    One of this kind is Hamlet:
    In sleep I heard him say 'Sweet Desdemona,
    Let us be wary, let us hide our loves;'
    And then, sir, would he gripe and wring my hand,
    Cry 'O sweet creature!' and then kiss me hard,
    As if he pluck'd up kisses by the roots
    That grew upon my lips: then laid his leg
    Over my thigh, and sigh'd, and kiss'd; and then
    Cried 'Cursèd fate that gave thee to the Moor!'

OTHELLO. Villain, be sure thou prove my love a whore,
    Be sure of it; give me the ocular proof:
    Make me to see't; or, at the least, so prove it,
    That the probation bear no hinge nor loop
    To hang a doubt on; or woe upon thy life!

IAGO. I see, sir, you are eaten up with passion:
    I do repent me that I put it to you.
    You would be satisfied?

OTHELLO.   Would! nay, I will.

IAGO. And may: but, how? how satisfied, my lord?
    Would you, the supervisor, grossly gape on—
    Behold her topp'd?

OTHELLO.   Death and damnation! O!

IAGO. But yet, I say,
    If imputation and strong circumstances,
    Which lead directly to the door of truth,
    Will give you satisfaction, you may have't.

OTHELLO. How may we try it further?

IAGO. You know, sometimes he walks four hours together
Here in the lobby.

OTHELLO. So she does as well.

IAGO. Be you and I behind an arras then;
Mark the encounter: if he love her not
And be not from his reason fall'n thereon,
Let me be no assistant for a state,
But keep a farm and carters.

OTHELLO. We will try it.

IAGO. I hear him coming: let's withdraw, my lord.

(They retire. Enter **HAMLET** *and* **DESDEMONA**, *and* **OPHELIA**, *attending.)*

HAMLET. I do beseech you
That by your virtuous means I may again
Exist, and be a member of his love
Whom I with all the office of my heart
Entirely honour.

OPHELIA. Here's a change indeed!

DESDEMONA. Trust me, I am glad on't
With all my heart; and it doth much content me
To hear him so inclined.
Be thou assured, good Hamlet, I will do
All my abilities in thy behalf.
His bed shall seem a school, his board a shrift;
I'll intermingle every thing he does
With Hamlet's suit: therefore be merry, Hamlet;
For thy solicitor shall rather die
Than give thy cause away.

OPHELIA. *[Aside]* I fear the trust my mistress puts him in.
Whom I will trust as I will adders fang'd.

DESDEMONA. Here comes my lord.

HAMLET. Madam, I'll take my leave.

DESDEMONA. Why, stay, and hear me speak.

HAMLET. Madam, not now: I am very ill at ease.
DESDEMONA. Well, do your discretion.

(*Exit* **HAMLET**. *Re-enter* **OTHELLO** *and* **IAGO**.)

IAGO. Ha! I like not that.
OTHELLO. What dost thou say?
IAGO. Nothing, my lord: or if—I know not what.
OTHELLO. Was not that Hamlet parted from my wife?
IAGO. Hamlet, my lord! No, sure, I cannot think it,
  That he would steal away so guilty-like,
  Seeing you coming.
OTHELLO. I do believe 'twas he.
IAGO. It may be, very likely.
OTHELLO. I heard thee say even now, thou likedst not that,
  When Hamlet left my wife: what didst not like?—
DESDEMONA. How now, my lord!
OTHELLO. *[Aside]* If she be false,—
IAGO. *[Aside]* Work on,
  My medicine, work! Thus credulous fools are caught;
  And many worthy and chaste dames even thus.

(*Exit.*)

DESDEMONA. I have been talking with a suitor here,
  A man that languishes in your displeasure.
OTHELLO. Who is't you mean?
DESDEMONA. Why, your lieutenant, Hamlet. Good my lord.
OTHELLO. Went he hence now?
DESDEMONA. Ay, sooth; so humbled
  That he hath left part of his grief with me,
  To suffer with him. Good love, call him back.
OTHELLO. Not now, sweet Desdemona; some other time.
DESDEMONA. But shall't be shortly?
OTHELLO. The sooner, sweet, for you.
DESDEMONA. Shall't be to-night at supper?

OTHELLO. No, not to-night.

DESDEMONA. To-morrow dinner, then?

OTHELLO. I shall not dine at home.

DESDEMONA. Why, then, to-morrow night; or Tuesday morn;
On Tuesday noon, or night; on Wednesday morn:
I prithee, name the time,—

OTHELLO. Prithee, no more:
I do beseech thee, grant me this,
To leave me but a little to myself.

DESDEMONA. 'Las, what's the matter? what's the matter, husband?

OTHELLO. I have a pain upon my forehead here.

DESDEMONA. *[Offering her handkerchief]* Let me but bind it hard, within this hour
It will be well.

OTHELLO. Your napkin is too little:

(He puts the handkerchief from him, and it drops.)

Let it alone. Come, I'll go in with you.

DESDEMONA. I am very sorry that you are not well.

(Exeunt. Re-enter **IAGO**. *Enter* **BIANCA** *with a bundle of costumes.)*

IAGO. How now, Bianca!

BIANCA. Save you, Iago!

IAGO. What make you from home? I' faith, sweet love, I was coming to your house.

BIANCA. Where shall we meet i' the morning?

IAGO. At my lodging.

BIANCA. I'll be with thee betimes.

IAGO. Go to; farewell.

(Exeunt, severally. Re-enter **OPHELIA**. *She recovers the handkerchief.)*

OPHELIA. I am glad I have found this napkin:

This was her first remembrance from the Moor:
For he conjured her she should ever keep it,
That she reserves it evermore about her
To kiss and talk to.
'Tis that the Moor first gave to Desdemona;
That which my father often bid me steal.

(Enter **HAMLET**.*)*

HAMLET. The fair Ophelia! Nymph, in thy orisons
Be all my sins remember'd.

OPHELIA. My lord, I have remembrances of yours,
That I have longèd long to re-deliver;
I pray you, now receive them.

HAMLET.   No, not I;
I never gave you aught.

OPHELIA. My honour'd lord, you know right well you did:
Take these again; for to the noble mind
Rich gifts wax poor when givers prove unkind.
There, my lord.

HAMLET. I did love you once.

OPHELIA. Indeed, my lord, you made me believe so.

HAMLET. You should not have believed me; for virtue cannot so inoculate our old stock but we shall relish of it: I loved you not.

OPHELIA. I was the more deceived.

HAMLET. Get thee to a nunnery: why wouldst thou be a breeder of sinners? If thou dost marry, I'll give thee this plague for thy dowry: be thou as chaste as ice, as pure as snow, thou shalt not escape calumny. Get thee to a nunnery, go: farewell. Or, if thou wilt needs marry, marry a fool; for wise men know well enough what monsters you make of them. To a nunnery, go, and quickly too. Farewell.

OPHELIA. O, help him, you sweet heavens!

*(***OPHELIA** *withdraws.)*

HAMLET. To be, or not to be: that is the question:
   Whether 'tis nobler in the mind to suffer
   The slings and arrows of outrageous fortune,
   Or to take arms against a sea of troubles,
   And by opposing end them? To die: to sleep;
   No more; and by a sleep to say we end
   The heart-ache and the thousand natural shocks
   That flesh is heir to, 'tis a consummation
   Devoutly to be wish'd. To die, to sleep;
   To sleep: perchance to dream: ay, there's the rub;
   For in that sleep of death what dreams may come
   When we have shuffled off this mortal coil,
   Must give us pause: there's the respect
   That makes calamity of so long life;
   For who would bear the whips and scorns of time,
   The oppressor's wrong, the proud man's contumely,
   The pangs of despised love, the law's delay,
   When he himself might his quietus make
   With a bare bodkin? who would fardels bear,
   To grunt and sweat under a weary life,
   But that the dread of something after death,
   The undiscover'd country from whose bourn
   No traveller returns, puzzles the will
   And makes us rather bear those ills we have
   Than fly to others that we know not of?
   Thus conscience does make cowards of us all;
   And enterprises of great pith and moment
   With this regard their currents turn awry,
   And lose the name of action.—Soft you now!

   (Seeing someone coming, **HAMLET** *withdraws.*
   OTHELLO *enters.)*

OTHELLO. O, my offence is rank it smells to heaven;
   As, I confess, it is my nature's plague
   To spy into abuses, and oft my jealousy

Shapes faults that are not—
O, beware, my soul, of jealousy;
It is the green-eyed monster which doth mock
The meat it feeds on; that cuckold lives in bliss
Who, certain of his fate, loves not his wronger;
But, O, what damnèd minutes tells he o'er
Who dotes, yet doubts, suspects, yet strongly loves!
And, like a man to double business bound,
I stand in pause where I shall first begin,
And both neglect.
O curse of marriage,
That we can call these delicate creatures ours,
And not their appetites! I had rather be a toad,
And live upon the vapour of a dungeon,
Than keep a corner in the thing I love
For others' uses. But, beshrew my jealousy!
O wretched state! O bosom black as death!
O limèd soul, that, struggling to be free,
Art more engaged! Help, angels! Make assay!
Bow, stubborn knees; and, heart with strings of steel,
Be soft as sinews of the newborn babe!
All may be well.

*(**OTHELLO** kneels. Re-enter **HAMLET**, drawing his sword.)*

HAMLET. Now might I do it pat, now he is praying;
And now I'll do't. And so he goes to heaven;
And so am I revenged. That would be scann'd:
A villain kills my father; and for that,
I, his sole son, do this same villain send
To heaven.
O, this is hire and salary, not revenge.
He took my father grossly, full of bread;
With all his crimes broad blown, as flush as May;
And how his audit stands who knows save heaven?

But in our circumstance and course of thought,
'Tis heavy with him: and am I then revenged,
To take him in the purging of his soul,
When he is fit and season'd for his passage?
No!

(OTHELLO rises.)

OTHELLO. Pray can I not,
Though inclination be as sharp as will:
My stronger guilt defeats my strong intent;
My words fly up, my thoughts remain below:
Words without thoughts never to heaven go.

(Exit.)

HAMLET. Up, sword; and know thou a more horrid hent:
When he is drunk asleep, or in his rage,
At gaming, swearing, or about some act
That has no relish of salvation in't;
Then trip him, that his heels may kick at heaven,
And that his soul may be as damn'd and black
As his own face. And hell, whereto it goes.

(Exit **HAMLET**. *Re-enter* **OPHELIA**.*)*

OPHELIA. O, what a noble mind is here o'erthrown!
That suck'd the honey of his music vows,
Now see that noble and most sovereign reason,
Like sweet bells jangled, out of tune and harsh.

(Enter **IAGO**.*)*

IAGO. How now! what do you here alone?
OPHELIA. Do not you chide; I have a thing for you.
IAGO. A thing for me?
OPHELIA. What will you give me now
For the same handkerchief?
IAGO. What handkerchief?
OPHELIA. Why, that the Moor first gave to Desdemona;
That which so often you did bid me steal.

IAGO. Hast stol'n it from her?

OPHELIA. No, faith; she let it drop by negligence.
And, to the advantage, I, being here, took't up.
Look, here it is.

IAGO. A good wench; give it me.

OPHELIA. What will you do with 't, that you have been so earnest
To have me filch it?

IAGO. *[Snatching it]* Why, what's that to you?

OPHELIA. If it be not for some purpose of import,
Give't me again: poor lady, she'll run mad
When she shall lack it.

IAGO. Be not acknown on 't; I have use for it.
Go, leave me.

(Exit **OPHELIA.** *Re-enter* **OTHELLO**; **IAGO** *hides the handkerchief.)*

OTHELLO. Ha! ha! false to me?

IAGO. Why, how now, general! no more of that.

OTHELLO. Avaunt! be gone! thou hast set me on the rack:
I swear 'tis better to be much abused
Than but to know't a little.

IAGO. How now, my lord!
She may be honest yet. Tell me but this,
Have you not sometimes seen a handkerchief
Spotted with strawberries in your wife's hand?

OTHELLO. I gave her such a one; 'twas my first gift.

IAGO. I know not that; but such a handkerchief—
I am sure it was your wife's—did I to-day
See Hamlet wipe his beard with.

OTHELLO. If it be that—

IAGO. If it be that, or any that was hers,
It speaks against her with the other proofs.

OTHELLO. Now do I see 'tis true. Look here, Iago;
All my fond love thus do I blow to heaven.

'Tis gone.
Arise, black vengeance, from thy hollow cell!
Yield up, O love, thy crown and hearted throne
To tyrannous hate! Swell, bosom, with thy fraught,
For 'tis of aspics' tongues!

IAGO. Yet be content.

OTHELLO. O, blood, Iago, blood!

IAGO. Patience, I say; your mind perhaps may change.

OTHELLO. O, that the slave had forty thousand lives!
One is too poor, too weak for my revenge.

(Exit.)

IAGO. I have rubb'd this old quat almost to the sense,
And he grows angry. Now, whether he kill Hamlet,
Or Hamlet him, or each do kill the other,
Every way makes my gain.

(Taking out the handkerchief.)

I will in Hamlet's lodging lose this napkin,
And let him find it. Trifles light as air
Are to the jealous confirmations strong
As proofs of holy writ: this may do something.
Dangerous conceits are, in their natures, poisons.
'Tis so, indeed: if such tricks as these strip him out of his lieutenantry.

(Exit.)

ACT III – The Play-Within-The-Play

SCENE 1 – A room in the castle.

(Enter **HORATIO**, **MARCELLUS**, *and* **HAMLET**, *toying with his new-found handkerchief.)*

HAMLET. I have of late—but wherefore I know not—lost all my mirth, forgone all custom of exercises; and indeed it goes so heavily with my disposition that this goodly frame, the earth, seems to me a sterile promontory, this most excellent canopy, the air, look you, this brave o'erhanging firmament, this majestical roof fretted with golden fire, why, it appears no other thing to me than a foul and pestilent congregation of vapours. What a piece of work is a man! how noble in reason! how infinite in faculty! in form and moving how express and admirable! in action how like an angel! in apprehension how like a god! the beauty of the world! the paragon of animals! And yet, to me, what is this quintessence of dust? man delights not me: no, nor woman neither, though by your smiling you seem to say so.

MARCELLUS. My lord, there was no such stuff in my thoughts.

HAMLET. Why did you laugh then, when I said 'man delights not me'?

MARCELLUS. To think, my lord, if you delight not in man, what lenten entertainment the players shall receive from you: Iago coted them on the way; and hither are they coming, to offer you service.

HAMLET. He that plays the king shall be welcome; his majesty shall have tribute of me; the adventurous knight shall use his foil and target; the lover shall not sigh gratis; the humourous man shall end his part in peace; the clown shall make those laugh whose lungs are tickled o' the sere; and the lady shall say her mind freely, or the blank verse shall halt for't. What players are they?

MARCELLUS. Even those you were wont to take delight in, the tragedians of the city.

HAMLET. The best actors in the world, either for tragedy, comedy, history, pastoral, pastoral-comical, historical-pastoral, tragical-historical, tragical-comical-historical-pastoral, scene individable, or poem unlimited: Seneca cannot be too heavy, nor Plautus too light. For the law of writ and the liberty, these are the only men.

(Flourish of trumpets within.)

MARCELLUS. There are the players.

*(**HORATIO** snatches away **HAMLET**'s handkerchief.)*

HORATIO. Lord Hamlet, whence came this?

*(He tosses the handkerchief to **MARCELLUS**, who also keeps it from him.)*

MARCELLUS. This is some token from a newer friend.
HORATIO. Is't come to this? Well, well.
HAMLET. Go to, go to!

(Takes back his handkerchief.)

Throw your vile guesses in the devil's teeth,
From whence you have them. You are jealous now
That this is from some mistress.

MARCELLUS. Why, whose is it?

HAMLET. I know not, sir: I found it in my chamber.

HORATIO. A likely piece of work, that you should find it in your chamber, and not know who left it there!

*(Enter **IAGO**.)*

IAGO. The actors are come hither, my lord.

(Enter four or five **PLAYERS**, *among them,* **BIANCA** *as the* **PLAYER QUEEN**.*)*

HAMLET. You are welcome, masters; welcome, all. I am glad to see thee well. Welcome, good friends. O, my old friend! thy face is valenced since I saw thee last: comest thou to beard me in Denmark? What, my young lady and mistress! By'r lady, your ladyship is nearer to heaven than when I saw you last, by the altitude of a chopine. Pray God, your voice, like a piece of uncurrent gold, be not cracked within the ring. Masters, you are all welcome. *[to* **IAGO***]* Good my lord, will you see the players well bestowed? Do you hear, let them be well used; for they are the abstract and brief chronicles of the time: after your death you were better have a bad epitaph than their ill report while you live.

IAGO. My lord, I will use them according to their desert.

HAMLET. God's bodykins, man, much better: use every man after his desert, and who should 'scape whipping? Use them after your own honour and dignity: the less they deserve, the more merit is in your bounty. Take them in.

IAGO. Come, sirs.

HAMLET. Follow him, friends: we'll hear a play to-morrow.

(Exit **IAGO**, **HORATIO** *and* **MARCELLUS** *with all the* **PLAYERS** *but the* **FIRST**.*)*

Dost thou hear me, old friend; can you play the Murder of Gonzago?

FIRST PLAYER. Ay, my lord.

HAMLET. We'll ha't to-morrow night. You could, for a need, study a speech of some dozen or sixteen lines, which I would set down and insert in't, could you not?

FIRST PLAYER. Ay, my lord.

HAMLET. Very well. Follow that lord; and look you mock him not.

(Exit **FIRST PLAYER**.*)*

I have heard
That guilty creatures sitting at a play

Have by the very cunning of the scene
Been struck so to the soul that presently
They have proclaim'd their malefactions;
For murder, though it have no tongue, will speak
With most miraculous organ. I'll have these players
Play something like the murder of my father
Before Othello: I'll observe his looks;
I'll tent him to the quick: if he but blench,
I know my course. The spirit that I have seen
May be the devil: and the devil hath power
To assume a pleasing shape; yea, and perhaps
Out of my weakness and my melancholy,
As he is very potent with such spirits,
Abuses me to damn me: I'll have grounds
More relative than this: the play 's the thing
Wherein I'll catch the conscience of the king.

(Exit.)

SCENE 2 – A corridor in the castle.

(Enter **DESDEMONA** *and* **OPHELIA**.*)*

DESDEMONA. Where should I lose that handkerchief, Ophelia?

OPHELIA. I know not, madam.

DESDEMONA. Believe me, I had rather have lost my purse
Full of crusadoes: and, but my noble Moor
Is true of mind and made of no such baseness
As jealous creatures are, it were enough
To put him to ill thinking.

OPHELIA.   Is he not jealous?

DESDEMONA. Who, he? I think the sun where he was born
Drew all such humours from him.

(Exeunt.)

SCENE 3 – A hall in the castle.

> (*Enter* **HAMLET** *and* **PLAYERS**, *rehearsing;* **BIANCA** *as the* **PLAYER QUEEN**.)

PLAYER QUEEN. 'But who, O, who had seen the mobled queen—'

HAMLET. The mobled queen?

PLAYER QUEEN. 'Run barefoot up and down, threatening the flames
With bisson rheum; a clout upon that head
Where late the diadem stood,—'

HAMLET. Here's for your clout.

> (*Gives her* **DESDEMONA**'s *handkerchief.*)

PLAYER QUEEN.   'and for a robe,
About her lank and all o'er-teemèd loins,
A blanket, in the alarm of fear caught up;—'

HAMLET. *[Coaching her]* 'Zounds, girl, you're robb'd; for shame, put on your gown;
Your heart is burst, you have lost half your soul;

> (*Tying the handkerchief about her head for a kerchief.*)

Put your bonnet to his right use; 'tis for the head:
So, proceed you.

PLAYER QUEEN. 'But if the gods themselves did see her then—'

HAMLET. Pray you, no more.
These words, like daggers, enter in mine ears:
Speak the speech, I pray you, as I pronounced it to you, trippingly on the tongue: but if you mouth it, as many of your players do, I had as lief the town-crier spoke my lines. Nor do not saw the air too much with your hand, thus, but use all gently; for in the very torrent, tempest, and, as I may say, the whirlwind of passion, you must acquire and beget a temperance that may give it smoothness.

PLAYER QUEEN. I warrant your honour.

HAMLET. Be not too tame neither, but let your own discretion be your tutor: suit the action to the word, the word to the action; with this special o'erstep not the modesty of nature: for any thing so overdone is from the purpose of playing, whose end, both at the first and now, was and is, to hold, as 'twere, the mirror up to nature; to show virtue her own feature, scorn her own image, and the very age and body of the time his form and pressure. Go, make you ready.

(Exeunt **PLAYERS.** *Enter* **MARCELLUS.***)*

How now, my friend! Will the king hear this piece of work?

MARCELLUS. And the queen too, and that presently.

HAMLET. Bid the players make haste.

MARCELLUS. I will, my lord.

(Exeunt.)

***SCENE 4** – A corridor in the castle.*

*(Enter **OTHELLO** and **IAGO**.)*

IAGO. If I give my wife a handkerchief,—
OTHELLO. What then?
IAGO. Why, then, 'tis hers, my lord; and, being hers,
She may, I think, bestow't on any man.
OTHELLO. She is protectress of her honour too:
May she give that?
IAGO. Her honour is an essence that's not seen;
They have it very oft that have it not:
But, for the handkerchief,—
OTHELLO. Ay, what of that?
IAGO. That's not so good now.

(Exeunt.)

SCENE 5 – *A hall in the castle.*

(*Enter* **HAMLET**.)

HAMLET. What ho! Horatio!

(*Enter* **HORATIO**.)

HORATIO. Here, sweet lord, at your service.

HAMLET. There is a play to-night before the king;
One scene of it comes near the circumstance
Which I have told thee of my father's death:
I prithee, when thou seest that act afoot,
Observe Othello: if his occulted guilt
Do not itself unkennel in one speech,
It is a damnèd ghost that we have seen.

HORATIO. Well, my lord:
If he steal aught the whilst this play is playing,
And 'scape detecting, I will pay the theft.

(*Danish march; A flourish.*)

HAMLET. They are coming to the play; I must be idle:
Get you a place.

(*Enter* **OTHELLO**, **DESDEMONA**, **OPHELIA**, **IAGO**, *and others.*)

OTHELLO. How fares our cousin Hamlet?

HAMLET. Excellent, i' faith; of the chameleon's dish:
I eat the air, promise-crammed: you cannot feed capons so.

OTHELLO. Have you heard the argument? Is there no offence in 't?

HAMLET. No, no, they do but jest, poison in jest; no offence i' the world. 'Tis a knavish piece of work: but what o' that? your majesty and we that have free souls, it touches us not: let the galled jade wince, our withers are unwrung. *[To* **MARCELLUS**] Be the players ready?

MARCELLUS. Ay, my lord; they stay upon your patience.

(*Exeunt* **HAMLET** *and* **MARCELLUS**.)

OTHELLO. *[Aside to* **IAGO***]* There's something in his soul,
O'er which his melancholy sits on brood;
And I do doubt the hatch and the disclose
Will be some danger: which for to prevent,
I have in quick determination
Thus set it down: he shall with speed to England.

IAGO. *[Aside to* **OTHELLO***]* My lord, do as you please;
But, if you hold it fit, after the play
Let his queen mother all alone entreat him
And I'll be placed, so please you, in the ear
Of all their conference. If this find him not,
To England send him, or confine him where
Your wisdom best shall think.

(They take their seats. Re-enter **HAMLET***; he lies down at* **OPHELIA***'s feet.)*

HAMLET. Lady, shall I lie in your lap?

OPHELIA. You are merry, my lord.

HAMLET. O God, your only jig-maker. What should a man do but be merry? for, look you, how cheerfully my mother looks, and my father died within these two hours.

OPHELIA. Nay, 'tis twice two months, my lord.

HAMLET. So long? Nay then, let the devil wear black, for I'll have a suit of sables. O heavens! die two months ago, and not forgotten yet? Then there's hope a great man's memory may outlive his life half a year.

DESDEMONA. Come hither, my dear Hamlet, sit by me.

IAGO. *[To* **OTHELLO***]* O, ho! do you mark that?

OTHELLO. *[To* **DESDEMONA***]* Pray, chuck, come hither.

DESDEMONA. What is the matter?

OTHELLO. I have a salt and sorry rheum offends me;
Lend me thy handkerchief.

DESDEMONA. Here, my lord.

OTHELLO. That which I gave you.

DESDEMONA. I have it not about me.

OTHELLO. Not?

DESDEMONA. No, indeed, my lord.

OTHELLO. That is a fault.

That handkerchief
Did an Egyptian to my mother give;
She was a charmer, and could almost read
The thoughts of people: she told her, while she kept it,
'Twould make her amiable and subdue my father
Entirely to her love, but if she lost it
Or made gift of it, my father's eye
Should hold her loathèd and his spirits should hunt
After new fancies: she, dying, gave it me;
And bid me, when my fate would have me wive,
To give it her. I did so: and take heed on't;
To lose't or give't away were such perdition
As nothing else could match.

(Hautboys play. The dumb-show enters.)

(Enter a King and a Queen, very lovingly; the Queen embracing him. She kneels, and makes show of protestation unto him. He takes her up, and declines his head upon her neck: lays him down upon a bank of flowers. She, seeing him asleep, leaves him. Anon comes in a fellow, takes off his crown, kisses it, and pours poison in the King's ears, and exits. The Queen returns, finds the King dead, and makes passionate action. The Poisoner, with some two or three Mutes, comes in again, seeming to lament with her. The dead body is carried away. The Poisoner woos the Queen with gifts. She seems loath and unwilling awhile, but in the end, accepts his love.)

DESDEMONA. Is't possible?

OTHELLO. 'Tis true: there's magic in the web of it.

DESDEMONA. Then would to God that I had never seen't!

OTHELLO. Ha!

(Exit the dumb-show.)

OPHELIA. Belike this show imports the argument of the play.

*(Enter two **PLAYERS**, King and Queen; The **PLAYER QUEEN**, like Desdemona, carries a handkerchief, which she flourishes when speaking.)*

PLAYER KING. Full thirty times hath Phoebus' cart gone round
 Neptune's salt wash and Tellus' orbèd ground,
 Since love our hearts and Hymen did our hands
 Unite commutual in most sacred bands.

> **OTHELLO.** *[to **DESDEMONA**]*
> Is't lost? is't gone? speak, is it out o' the way?

PLAYER QUEEN. So many journeys may the sun and moon
 Make us again count o'er ere love be done!

> **DESDEMONA.** *[to **OTHELLO**]* It is not lost; but what an if it were?
>
> **OTHELLO.** How!
>
> **DESDEMONA.** I say, it is not lost.

PLAYER KING. But, woe is me, you are so sick of late,
 So far from cheer and from your former state.

> **OTHELLO.** *[to **DESDEMONA**]* Fetch't, let me see't.
>
> **DESDEMONA.** Why, so I can, sir, but I will not now.

PLAYER KING. Faith, I must leave thee, love, and shortly too;
 My operant powers their functions leave to do:

And thou shalt live in this
  fair world behind,
Honour'd, beloved; and
  haply one as kind
For husband shalt thou—
PLAYER KING.   O, confound the rest!
Such love must needs be
  treason in my breast:
In second husband let me
  be accurst!
None wed the second but
  who kill'd the first.

                    HAMLET. *[Aside]* Wormwood,
                              wormwood.

PLAYER KING. I do believe
  you think what now you
  speak;
But what we do deter-
  mine oft we break.
So think thou wilt no
  second husband wed;
But die thy thoughts
  when thy first lord is
  dead.
PLAYER QUEEN. Both here
  and hence pursue me last-
  ing strife,
If, once a widow, ever I be
  wife!

                    HAMLET. If she should break
                              it now!

PLAYER KING. 'Tis deeply sworn. Sweet, leave me here awhile;
My spirits grow dull, and fain I would beguile
The tedious day with sleep.

(Sleeps.)

PLAYER QUEEN.   Sleep rock thy brain,
And never come mischance between us twain!

(Daubs his brow with her handkerchief, and exit.)

HAMLET. Madam, how like you this play?

DESDEMONA. The lady protests too much, methinks.

HAMLET. O, but she'll keep her word.

IAGO. *[Aside to* **OTHELLO***]* And did you see the handkerchief?

OTHELLO. Was that mine?

IAGO. Yours by this hand: and to see how he prizes his foolish mother your wife! she gave it him, and he hath given it this whore.

(Enter **LUCIANUS.***)*

HAMLET. This is one Lucianus, general to the king. He poisons him i' the garden for's estate.

LUCIANUS. Thoughts black, hands apt, drugs fit, and time agreeing; Confederate season, else no creature seeing; Thou mixture rank, of midnight weeds collected, With Hecate's ban thrice blasted, thrice infected, Thy natural magic and dire property, On wholesome life usurp immediately.

(Pours the poison into the sleeper's ear, and exits.)

(The **PLAYER QUEEN** *enters, weeping for the dead King, gesticulating with her handkerchief.)*

OPHELIA. The king rises.

OTHELLO. Fetch me the handkerchief: my mind misgives.

DESDEMONA. Come, come.

OTHELLO. The handkerchief!

DESDEMONA. I have sent to bid Hamlet come speak with you.

OTHELLO. The handkerchief!

DESDEMONA. I pray, talk me of Hamlet.

OTHELLO. The handkerchief!

DESDEMONA. In sooth, you are to blame.

OTHELLO. Away!

HAMLET. What, frighted with false fire!
DESDEMONA. How fares my lord?
IAGO. Give o'er the play.
OTHELLO. By heaven, that should be my handkerchief!

(**OTHELLO** *seizes the* **PLAYER QUEEN**'s *handkerchief; She struggles to keep it; He strikes her to the ground.*)

Give me some light: away!
ALL. Lights, lights, lights!
OPHELIA. Is not this man jealous?
DESDEMONA. I ne'er saw this before.
Sure, there's some wonder in this handkerchief:
I am most unhappy in the loss of it.

(*Exeunt all but* **HAMLET** *and* **HORATIO**.)

HAMLET. O good Horatio,
I'll take the ghost's word for a thousand pound.
Didst perceive?
HORATIO. Very well, my lord.
HAMLET. Upon the talk of the poisoning?
HORATIO. I did very well note him.

(*Re-enter* **MARCELLUS**.)

MARCELLUS. Good my lord, vouchsafe me a word with you.
HAMLET. Sir, a whole history.
MARCELLUS. The king, sir,—
HAMLET. Ay, sir, what of him?
MARCELLUS. Is in his retirement marvellous distempered. The queen, your mother, in most great affliction of spirit, hath sent me to you. Your behavior hath struck her into amazement and admiration.
HAMLET. O wonderful son, that can so astonish a mother! But is there no sequel at the heels of this mother's admiration? Impart.
MARCELLUS. She desires to speak with you in her closet, ere you go to bed.
HAMLET. We shall obey, were she ten times our mother.

(*Exeunt.*)

ACT IV – The Murder in the Closet

SCENE 1 – Royal antechamber.

(*Enter* **OTHELLO** *and* **IAGO**.)

OTHELLO. How shall I murder him, Iago?

IAGO. Did you perceive how he laughed at his vice?

OTHELLO. I would have him nine years a-killing. A fine woman! a fair woman! a sweet woman!
O, that incestuous, that adulterate beast.

IAGO. O, 'tis foul in her.

OTHELLO. Get me some poison, Iago; this night: I'll not expostulate with her, lest her body and beauty unprovide my mind again: this night, Iago.

IAGO. And for Hamlet, let me be his undertaker: you shall hear more by midnight.

OTHELLO. Within these three days let me hear thee say
That Hamlet's not alive.

IAGO. My friend is dead;
'Tis done at your request: But let her live.

OTHELLO. Damn her, lewd minx! O, damn her!
Let not the royal bed of Denmark be
A couch for luxury and damnèd incest.

IAGO. Nay, you must forget that.

OTHELLO. Hang her! I will chop her into messes: cuckold me!

DESDEMONA. *[Within]* What noise? Who's there? Othello?

OTHELLO. Ay, Desdemona.

(*Enter* **DESDEMONA**.)

DESDEMONA. Will you come to bed, my lord?

OTHELLO. Have you pray'd to-night, Desdemona?

DESDEMONA. Ay, my lord.

OTHELLO. If you bethink yourself of any crime
Unreconciled as yet to heaven and grace,
Solicit for it straight.

DESDEMONA. Alas, my lord, what do you mean by that?

OTHELLO. That handkerchief which I so loved and gave thee
Thou gavest to Hamlet.

DESDEMONA. No, by my life and soul!

OTHELLO. By heaven, I saw my handkerchief to-night.
O perjured woman! thou dost stone my heart,
And makest me call what I intend to do
A murder, which I thought a sacrifice.

DESDEMONA. Talk you of killing?

OTHELLO. Ay, I do.

DESDEMONA. Then heaven
Have mercy on me!

OTHELLO. Amen, with all my heart!

DESDEMONA. If you say so, I hope you will not kill me.

OTHELLO. I saw the handkerchief.

DESDEMONA. He found it then;—

OTHELLO. *[Striking her]* Devil!

DESDEMONA. I have not deserved this.

OTHELLO. Get you to bed on the instant; I will be returned forthwith: dismiss your attendant there: look it be done.

DESDEMONA. I will, my lord.

OTHELLO. Out of my sight!

DESDEMONA. I will not stay to offend you.

(*Exit.*)

OTHELLO. *[to* **IAGO**] Come, go with me apart; I will withdraw,

> To furnish me with some swift means of death
> For the fair devil. Now art thou my lieutenant.

IAGO. I am your own for ever.

OTHELLO. O bloody, bawdy villain!
> Remorseless, treacherous, lecherous, kindless villain!

IAGO. My lord, he's going to his mother's closet:
> Behind the arras I'll convey myself,
> To serve your purpose; Fare you well, my liege:
> I'll call upon you ere you go to bed,
> And tell you what is done.

> *(Exit* **OTHELLO.***)*

>   This is the night
> That either makes me or fordoes me quite.

> *(Enter* **BIANCA** *in the* **GHOST** *disguise.)*

BIANCA. I do not find that thou dealest justly with me.

IAGO. How now, Bianca! What do you mean by this haunting of me?

BIANCA. Let the devil and his dam haunt you! I have been to-night exceedingly well cudgelled; and I think the issue will be, I shall have so much experience for my pains.

IAGO. Well; go to; very well.

BIANCA. Very well! go to! I cannot go to, man; nor 'tis not very well: nay, I think it is scurvy, and begin to find myself fobbed in it.

IAGO. Very well.

BIANCA. I tell you 'tis not very well. Every day thou daffest me with some device, Iago; and I will indeed no longer endure it, nor am I yet persuaded to put up in peace what already I have foolishly suffered.

IAGO. Will you hear me, Bianca?

BIANCA. Faith, I have heard too much, for your words and performances are no kin together.

IAGO. You have said now.

BIANCA. Ay, and said nothing but what I protest intendment of doing. I will give over my suit and repent my unlawful solicitation:

(*Removes the* **GHOST** *costume; Gives it to* **IAGO**.)

There; give it your hobby-horse: I was a fine fool to take it.

(*Exit.*)

IAGO. How now, my sweet Bianca! how now! how now! Faith, I must after her; she'll rail in the street else.— Goats and monkeys!

(*Exit.*)

SCENE 2 – *Another part of the castle.*

(Enter **HAMLET**.*)*

HAMLET. 'Tis now the very witching time of night,
When churchyards yawn and hell itself breathes out
Contagion to this world: now could I drink hot blood,
And do such bitter business as the day
Would quake to look on. Soft! now to my mother.
Let me be cruel, not unnatural:
I will speak daggers to her, but use none.

(Exit.)

SCENE 3 – *The queen's closet.*

(Enter **DESDEMONA** *and* **OPHELIA**.*)*

DESDEMONA. Lay on my bed my wedding sheets, Ophelia.
OPHELIA. Good madam, what's the matter with my lord?
DESDEMONA. He says he will return incontinent:
    He hath commanded me to go to bed,
    And bade me to dismiss you.
OPHELIA.   Dismiss me!
DESDEMONA. It was his bidding: therefore, good Ophelia,
    Give me my nightly wearing, and adieu:
    We must not now displease him.
    Prithee, unpin me.

(Sits for **OPHELIA** *to unpin her.)*

    My mother had a maid call'd Barbara:
    She was in love, and he she loved proved mad
    And did forsake her: she had a song of 'willow;'
    An old thing 'twas, but it express'd her fortune,
    And she died singing it: that song to-night
    Will not go from my mind; I have much to do,
    But to go hang my head all at one side,
    And sing it like poor Barbara.
    [Singing] The poor soul sat sighing
    by a sycamore tree,
    Sing all a green willow:
DESDEMONA & OPHELIA. *[Singing] Her hand on her bosom,*
    her head on her knee,
    Sing willow, willow, willow:

	DESDEMONA. There is a willow grows aslant a brook,
	That shows his hoar leaves in the glassy stream;
	There with fantastic garlands did she come
OPHELIA. *[Singing] The fresh streams ran by her,*	Of crow-flowers, nettles, daisies, and long purples
and murmur'd her moans;	That liberal shepherds give a grosser name,
Sing willow, willow, willow;	But our cold maids do dead men's fingers call them:
	There, on the pendent boughs her coronet weeds
Her salt tears fell from her,	Clambering to hang, an envious sliver broke;
and soften'd the stones;	When down her weedy trophies and herself
Sing willow, willow, willow;	Fell in the weeping brook. Her clothes spread wide;
	And, mermaid-like, awhile they bore her up:
I call'd my love false love;	Which time she chanted snatches of old tunes;
but what said he then?	As one incapable of her own distress,
Sing willow, willow, willow:	Or like a creature native and indued
	Unto that element: but long it could not be
If I court moe women,	Till that her garments, heavy with their drink,
you'll couch with moe men!	Pull'd the poor wretch from her melodious lay
Sing all a green willow:	To muddy death.

(Enter IAGO.*)*

DESDEMONA. *[Singing] Let nobody blame him;*
his scorn I approve,—

OPHELIA. Nay, that's not next.—

DESDEMONA. So, get thee gone; good night:
Iago to-night watches on the court of guard.

IAGO. Bestow this place on us a little while.
For we have closely sent for Hamlet hither:
Prithee, hie thee; he'll come anon:—

(Exit OPHELIA.*)*

DESDEMONA. What tidings can you tell me of my son?

IAGO. But that he's well and will be shortly here;
He will come straight. Look you lay home to him:
Tell him his pranks have been too broad to bear with,
And that your grace hath screen'd and stood between
Much heat and him. I'll sconce me even here.
Pray you, be round with him.

HAMLET. *[Within]* Mother, mother, mother!

DESDEMONA. I'll warrant you,
Fear me not: withdraw, I hear him coming.

(IAGO *hides behind the arras. Enter* HAMLET.*)*

HAMLET. Now, mother, what's the matter?

DESDEMONA. Hamlet, thou hast thy father much offended.

HAMLET. Mother, you have my father much offended.

DESDEMONA. Come, come, you answer with an idle tongue.

HAMLET. Go, go, you question with a wicked tongue.

DESDEMONA. Why, how now, Hamlet!

HAMLET. What's the matter now?

DESDEMONA. Have you forgot me?

HAMLET. No, by the rood, not so:
You are the queen, your husband's general's wife;

And—would it were not so!—you are my mother.

DESDEMONA. Nay, then, I'll set those to you that can speak.

HAMLET. Come, come, and sit you down; you shall not budge;
You go not till I set you up a glass
Where you may see the inmost part of you.

DESDEMONA. What wilt thou do? thou wilt not murder me?
Help, help, ho!

HAMLET. Leave wringing of your hands: peace! sit you down,
And let me wring your heart; for so I shall,
If it be made of penetrable stuff,—

DESDEMONA. What have I done, that thou darest wag thy tongue
In noise so rude against me?

HAMLET. Such an act
That blurs the grace and blush of modesty,
Calls virtue hypocrite, makes marriage-vows
As false as dicers' oaths:—

DESDEMONA. Hark! who is't that knocks?

HAMLET. It's the wind.

(Enter **IAGO** *as the* **GHOST**.*)*

GHOST. Hamlet, Hamlet!

HAMLET. What noise? who calls on Hamlet?

DESDEMONA. Thy father, in his habit as he lived!

HAMLET. He is here even now; he haunts me in every place.
Save me, and hover o'er me with your wings,
You heavenly guards! What would your gracious figure?
Do you not come your tardy son to chide,
That, lapsed in time and passion, lets go by
The important acting of your dread command?
O, say!

GHOST. Do not forget: this visitation
Is but to whet thy almost blunted purpose.
But, look, amazement on thy mother sits:
O, step between her and her fighting soul:
Conceit in weakest bodies strongest works:
Speak to her, Hamlet.

HAMLET. How is it with you, lady?
Nay, stare not, mother: it is true, indeed.
It is an honest ghost, that let me tell you.

IAGO. *[Aside, drawing a sword]* Forth, my sword: he dies; and the impediment most profitably removed, without the which there were no expectation of my prosperity.

HAMLET. *[To* **DESDEMONA***]* Alas, how is't with you,
Your bedded hair, like life in excrements,
Starts up, and stands on end.
Whereon do you look?

DESDEMONA. On him, on him! Look you, how pale he glares!

(**GHOST** *stabs* **HAMLET**.)

HAMLET. That thrust had been mine enemy indeed,
But that my coat is better than thou know'st
I will make proof of thine.

(Draws, and wounds him.)

IAGO. O, I am slain!

HAMLET. If that thou be'st a devil, I cannot kill thee.

(**GHOST** *tries to flee.*)

DESDEMONA. Why, look you there! look, how it steals away!
Look, where he goes, even now, out at the arras!

HAMLET. How now! a rat? Dead, for a ducat, dead!

(Makes a pass through the arras; **GHOST** *falls.)*

DESDEMONA. O me, what hast thou done?
HAMLET. Nay, I know not:
Is it the king?

DESDEMONA. O, what a rash and bloody deed is this!
HAMLET. A bloody deed! almost as bad, good mother,
  As kill a king, and marry with another.
DESDEMONA. As kill a king!
HAMLET.   Ay, lady, 'twas my word.
IAGO. O, help, ho! light! a surgeon!
HAMLET. What are you here that cry so grievously?

  (Lifting the **GHOST***'s mask, he discovers* **IAGO***.)*

  Iago? O, I am spoil'd, undone by villains!
DESDEMONA. 'Tis he:—O brave Iago, honest and just,—
HAMLET. O damn'd Iago! O inhuman dog!
  More fell than anguish, hunger, or the sea!
  This is thy work: Thou devil! O he deceives me
  Past thought! Kill men i' the dark!—O Spartan dog:
  The Moor's abused by this most villainous knave,
  And his reports have set the murder on.
IAGO. Demand me nothing: what you know, you know:
  From this time forth I never will speak word.
HAMLET. Thou wretched, rash, intruding fool, farewell!

  (Stabs him; **IAGO** *dies.)*

  I am sorry that I was deceived in him.
  I'll lug the guts into the neighbour room.
  Mother, good night. Indeed this counsellor
  Is now most still, most secret and most grave,
  Who was in life a foolish prating knave.
  Come, sir, to draw toward an end with you.
  Good night, mother.
  I will bestow him, and will answer well
  The death I gave him. So, again, good night.
  I must be cruel, only to be kind:
  Thus bad begins and worse remains behind.

  (Exit **HAMLET***, dragging* **IAGO***.)*

DESDEMONA. What, ho! help, help, help!

What, ho! no watch? no passage? murder! murder!

(Cry within: 'Help! help! Iago dead!')

Here, here! for heaven's sake, help me!

*(Enter **OTHELLO**.)*

Ah, my good lord, what have I seen to-night!

OTHELLO. What, strumpet? How does Hamlet?

DESDEMONA. Mad as the sea and wind, when both contend
Which is the mightier: in his lawless fit,
Behind the arras seeing something stir,
Whips out his rapier, cries, 'A rat, a rat!'
And, in this brainish apprehension, kills
The unseen good Iago.

OTHELLO.   O heavy deed!
It had been so with us, had we been there:
His liberty is full of threats to all;
To you yourself, to us, to every one.
Alas, how shall this bloody deed be answer'd?

GENTLEMAN. *[Within]* My lord, my lord! what, ho! my lord, my lord!

OTHELLO. Who's there?

(Noise within.)

DESDEMONA. Alack, what noise is this?

OTHELLO. Where are my Switzers? Let them guard the door.

(Enter another Gentleman.)

What is the matter?

GENTLEMAN.   Save yourself, my lord:
The ocean, overpeering of his list,
Eats not the flats with more impetuous haste
Than young Ophelia, in a riotous head,
O'erbears your officers.

(Noise within.)

OTHELLO. The doors are broke.

(Enter **OPHELIA**, *armed.)*

OPHELIA. O thou vile king,
   Give me my father!
DESDEMONA.   Calmly, good Ophelia.
OPHELIA. That drop of blood that's calm proclaims me bastard,
   Cries cuckold to my father, brands the harlot
   Even here, between the chaste unsmirchèd brow
   Of my true mother.
OTHELLO.   What is the cause, Ophelia,
   That thy rebellion looks so giant-like?
   Let her go, my queen; do not fear our person.
   Speak, lass.
OPHELIA. Where is my father?
OTHELLO.   Dead.
DESDEMONA.   But not by him.
OTHELLO. Let her demand her fill.
OPHELIA. How came he dead? I'll not be juggled with:
   To hell, allegiance! vows, to the blackest devil!
   Let come what comes; only I'll be revenged
   Most thoroughly for my father.

   *(***OTHELLO** *disarms* **OPHELIA**.*)*

OTHELLO. That I am guiltless of your father's death,
   And am most sensible in grief for it,
   It shall as level to your judgment pierce
   As day does to your eye.
   I pray you, go with me.
   And where the offence is let the great axe fall.

   (Exeunt.)

SCENE 4 – *The lobby of the castle.*

(*Enter* **HAMLET** *and* **HORATIO**, *dragging* **IAGO**'*s body;* **HAMLET** *pins a letter to the corpse with a dagger.*)

HAMLET. Safely stowed.
Alas, poor Iago! I knew him, Horatio: a fellow of infinite jest, of most excellent fancy: he hath borne me on his back a thousand times; and now, how abhorred in my imagination it is! my gorge rims at it. Where be your gibes now? your gambols? your songs? your flashes of merriment, that were wont to set the table on a roar? Not one now, to mock your own grinning? quite chap-fallen? Prithee, Horatio, tell me one thing.

HORATIO. What's that, my lord?

HAMLET. Dost thou think Alexander looked o' this fashion i' the earth?

HORATIO. E'en so.

HAMLET. And smelt so? pah!

HORATIO. E'en so, my lord.

HAMLET. Imperious Caesar, dead and turn'd to clay,
Might stop a hole to keep the wind away:
O, that that earth, which kept the world in awe,
Should patch a wall to expel the winter flaw!
But soft! but soft! aside: here comes the king.

(*Exeunt. Enter* **KING OTHELLO** *and* **OPHELIA**.)

OTHELLO. Now must your conscience my acquaintance seal,
And you must put me in your heart for friend,
Sith you have heard, and with a knowing ear,
That he which hath your noble father slain
Pursued my life.

OPHELIA.   It well appears:
And so have I a noble father lost;
Whose worth, if praises may go back again,
Stood challenger on mount of all the age

For his perfections: but my revenge will come.

OTHELLO. You shortly shall hear more:
　I loved your father, and we love ourself;
　And that, I hope, will teach you to imagine—

*(**OPHELIA** discovers the dead body.)*

OPHELIA. Do you see this, O God?

OTHELLO. O, horrible! O, horrible! most horrible!

OPHELIA. O, treble woe
　Fall ten times treble on that cursèd head,
　Whose wicked deed thy most ingenious sense
　Deprived thee of! Hold off the heavens awhile,
　Till I have caught him once more in mine arms.

*(Embracing the corpse; she discovers **HAMLET**'s letter.)*

What bloody business is this?

OTHELLO. What's the matter?

OPHELIA. There's a letter for you, sir.

OTHELLO. *[Reads]* 'High and mighty, to-morrow shall I beg leave to see your kingly eyes: when I shall, first asking your pardon thereunto, recount the occasion of my sudden and more strange revolt. In that and all things will we show our duty. HAMLET.'
　What should this mean?
　Or is it some abuse, and no such thing?

OPHELIA. I'm lost in it, my lord. But let him come;
　It warms the very sickness in my heart,
　That I shall live and tell him to his teeth,
　'Thus didest thou.'

OTHELLO. 　　　　　　If it be so, Ophelia—
　Will you be ruled by me?

OPHELIA. 　　　　　　　　Ay, my lord;
　So you will not o'errule me to a peace.

OTHELLO. To thine own peace. Ophelia, I will work him
　To an exploit, now ripe in my device,
　Under the which he shall not choose but fall:

> And for his death no wind of blame shall breathe,
> But even his mother shall uncharge the practise
> And call it accident.

OPHELIA. My lord, I will be ruled;
> The rather, if you could devise it so
> That I might be the organ.

OTHELLO. It falls right.
> You have been talk'd of for a quality
> Wherein, they say, you shine:
> And gave you such a masterly report
> For art and exercise in your defence
> And for your rapier most especially.

OPHELIA. Ay, my lord.
> I have been in continual practise.

OTHELLO. Now, out of this,—

OPHELIA. What out of this, my lord?

(**OTHELLO** *takes out a vial of poison.*)

OTHELLO. I bought an unction of a mountebank,
> So mortal that, but dip a knife in it,
> Where it draws blood no cataplasm so rare,
> Collected from all simples that have virtue
> Under the moon, can save the thing from death.
> We will bring you and he in fine together
> And wager on your heads: he, being remiss,
> Holding a weak supposal of your worth,
> Colleaguèd with the dream of his advantage,
> Will not peruse the foils; so that, with ease,
> Or with a little shuffling, you may choose
> A sword unbated, and in a pass of practise
> Requite him for your father.

OPHELIA. I will do't:
> And, for that purpose, I'll anoint my sword.

OTHELLO. Till then, in patience our proceeding be.
> An hour of quiet shortly shall we see.

(Exit **OPHELIA**.*)*

And for the queen, when she is hot and dry—
And that she calls for drink, I'll have prepared her
A chalice for the nonce, whereon but sipping
The leperous distilment: she must die.

(Exit.)

ACT V – The Duel in the Bed Chamber

SCENE 1 – *The castle grounds.*

(Enter **HAMLET** *and* **HORATIO**.*)*

HAMLET. But I am very sorry, good Horatio,
  That to Ophelia I forgot myself;
  For, by the image of my cause, I see
  The portraiture of hers: I'll court her favours.

HORATIO. Peace! who comes here?

(Enter **MARCELLUS**.*)*

MARCELLUS. Sweet lord, if your lordship were at leisure, I should impart a thing to you from his majesty.

HAMLET. I will receive it, sir, with all diligence of spirit.

MARCELLUS. Good my lord, his majesty bade me signify to you that he has laid a great wager on your head: sir, this is the matter,—You are not ignorant of what excellence Ophelia is—

HAMLET. I know a lad in Venice would have walked barefoot to Palestine for a touch of her nether lip.

MARCELLUS. I mean, sir, for her weapon; but in the imputation laid on her by the queen, in her meed she's unfellowed. The king, sir, hath laid, that in a dozen passes between yourself and her, she shall not exceed you three hits: and it would come to immediate trial, if your lordship would vouchsafe the answer.

HAMLET. If it please their majesties, 'tis the breathing time of night with me; let the foils be brought, the gentlewoman willing, and the king hold his purpose, I will win for him an I can; if not, I will gain nothing but my shame and the odd hits.

MARCELLUS. I commend my duty to your lordship.

(Exit **MARCELLUS**.*)*

HAMLET. Come, let us to the castle.

(Exeunt.)

SCENE 2 – *The royal bedchamber.*

(**DESDEMONA** *in bed asleep; a light burning; Enter* **OTHELLO**. *He kisses her.*)

OTHELLO. Ah balmy breath, that dost almost persuade
Justice to break her sword! One more, one more.
Be thus when thou art dead, and I will kill thee,
And love thee after. One more, and this the last:
Forth of my heart those charms, thine eyes, are blotted;
Thy bed, lust-stain'd, shall with lust's blood be spotted.

(**DESDEMONA** *wakes.*)

Look, if my gentle love be not raised up!

DESDEMONA. Who's there? Othello?

OTHELLO. How now, sweet queen!

DESDEMONA. My lord, what is your will?

OTHELLO. Let me see your eyes;
Look in my face.

DESDEMONA. What horrible fancy's this?
Alas, why gnaw you so your nether lip?
Some bloody passion shakes your very frame:
These are portents; but yet I hope, I hope,
They do not point on me.

OTHELLO. Hum!

DESDEMONA. And yet I fear you; for you are fatal then
When your eyes roll so: why I should fear I know not,
Since guiltiness I know not; but yet I feel I fear.

(*Enter* **MARCELLUS.**)

MARCELLUS. The prince and court and all are coming down.

(*Exit* **MARCELLUS.**)

DESDEMONA. How! the king in council!
In this time of the night!

OTHELLO. Come, Desdemona: 'tis the soldiers' life

To have their balmy slumbers waked with strife.

(Re-enter **MARCELLUS**, *with* **HAMLET**, **OPHELIA**, **HORATIO**, *Lords and Attendants.)*

The goodness of the night upon you, friends!
Good Hamlet, you are welcome. *[To* **OPHELIA***]* Welcome, mistress.

OPHELIA. *[To* **DESDEMONA***]* How do you, madam? how do you, my good lady?

DESDEMONA. Faith, half asleep.

HAMLET. *[To* **OTHELLO***]* Give me your pardon, sir: I've done you wrong;
But pardon't, as you are a gentleman.

OTHELLO. Why, 'tis a loving and a fair reply:
Be as ourself in Denmark. Madam, come;
This gentle and unforced accord of Hamlet
Sits smiling to my heart: in grace whereof,
No jocund health that Denmark drinks to-day,
But the great cannon to the clouds shall tell,
And the king's rouse the heavens all bruit again,
Re-speaking earthly thunder.

HAMLET. If virtue no delighted beauty lack,
Your majesty is far more fair than black.

OTHELLO. Ophelia, come, and take this hand from me.

(Puts **OPHELIA***'s hand into* **HAMLET***'s.)*

If I have any grace or power to move you,
This present reconciliation take;
For if he be not one that truly loves you,
That errs in ignorance and not in cunning,
I have no judgment in an honest face.

HAMLET. This presence knows,
And you must needs have heard, how I am punish'd
With sore distraction. What I have done,
That might your nature, honour and exception
Roughly awake, I here proclaim was madness.

OTHELLO. It is the very error of the moon;
> She comes more nearer earth than she was wont,
> And makes men mad.

HAMLET. I protest, in the sincerity of love and honest kindness.
> These bloody accidents must excuse my manners:
> But I am much to blame;
> I humbly do beseech you of your pardon
> For too much loving you.

OPHELIA. I do receive your offer'd love like love,
> And will not wrong it.

HAMLET. I embrace it freely;
> And will the general's wager frankly play.
> Give us the foils. Come on.

OPHELIA. Come, one for me.

OTHELLO. You know the wager?

HAMLET. Very well, my lord
> Your grace hath laid the odds o' the weaker side.

OTHELLO. I do not fear it; I have seen you both.

OPHELIA. This is too heavy, let me see another.

HAMLET. This likes me well. These foils have all a length?

(They prepare to play.)

MARCELLUS. Ay, my good lord.

OTHELLO. Set me the stoops of wine upon that table.
> If Hamlet give the first or second hit,
> The king shall drink to Hamlet's better breath;
> And let the kettle to the trumpet speak,
> 'Now the king dunks to Hamlet.' Come, begin:
> And you, the judges, bear a wary eye.

HAMLET. Come on, then.

OPHELIA. Come, my lord.

(They play.)

HAMLET. One.

OPHELIA. No.

HAMLET.   Judgment.

MARCELLUS. A hit, a very palpable hit.

OPHELIA.   Well; again.

OTHELLO. Stay; give me drink. My queen, this pearl is thine;

   (Drops an union in the cup.)

   Here's to thy health. Give her the cup.
   I'll see this bout first; set it by awhile.

HAMLET. Come.

   (They play.)

                              Another hit; what say you?

OPHELIA. A touch, a touch, I do confess.

OTHELLO. The queen carouses to thy fortune, Hamlet.

DESDEMONA. I dare not drink yet, husband; by and by.

OPHELIA. *[To* **OTHELLO***]* My lord, I'll hit him now.

OTHELLO.   I do not think't.

OPHELIA. *[Aside]* And yet 'tis almost 'gainst my conscience.

OTHELLO. Our son shall win.

DESDEMONA.   He's fat, and scant of breath.
   Here, Hamlet, take my napkin, rub thy brows.

HAMLET. Drink, ho! Fetch me a stoup of liquor.

DESDEMONA. Come, let me wipe thy face.

   (**DESDEMONA** *wipes his brow with her handkerchief;*
   HAMLET *takes her cup to drink.)*

OTHELLO. Hamlet, do not drink.

HAMLET. I will, my lord; I pray you, pardon me.

   (**HAMLET** *drinks.)*

OTHELLO. *[Aside]* It is the poison'd cup: it is too late.

HAMLET. Come, for the third, Ophelia: you but dally;
   I pray you, pass with your best violence;
   I am afeard you make a wanton of me.

OPHELIA. You mock me, sir.

HAMLET. I mock you! no, by heaven.

OPHELIA. Say you so? come on.

(They play.)

MARCELLUS. Nothing, neither way.

OPHELIA. Have at you now!

*(**OPHELIA** lunges at him; in the scuffling, they change rapiers, and **HAMLET** wounds **OPHELIA**; Enraged, she drops her rapier and grapples with him.)*

The devil take thy soul!

HAMLET. Thou pray'st not well.
I prithee, take thy fingers from my throat.

OTHELLO. Part them; they are incensed.

(Attendants part them.)

HAMLET. Nay, come, again.

*(**HAMLET** falls.)*

MARCELLUS. Look to the prince there, ho!

*(**OPHELIA** falls.)*

HORATIO. They bleed on both sides. How is it, my lord?

MARCELLUS. How is't, Ophelia?

OPHELIA. Why, as a woodcock to mine own springe, Marcellus;
I am justly kill'd with mine own treachery.

*(**DESDEMONA** tastes the poisoned drink, spits it out.)*

HAMLET. How does the queen?

OTHELLO. She swounds to see them bleed.

DESDEMONA. No, no, the drink, the drink,—O my dear Hamlet,—
The drink, the drink! it is poison'd.

HAMLET. O villainy! Ho! let the door be lock'd:
Treachery! Seek it out.

OPHELIA. It is here, Hamlet:

The treacherous instrument is in thy hand,
Unbated and envenom'd: the foul practise
Hath turn'd itself on me, lo, here I lie,
Never to rise again:
I can no more: the king, the king's to blame.

HAMLET. The point!—envenom'd too! Then, venom, to thy work.

*(Charges at the King; but in **HAMLET**'s weakened state, **OTHELLO** easily beats aside the attack.)*

ALL. Treason! treason!

OTHELLO. Wrench his sword from him.
Thy cup is poison'd: Hamlet, thou art slain;
No medicine in the world can do thee good;
In thee there is not half an hour of life.

DESDEMONA. Alas! he is betray'd and I undone.

OTHELLO. Out, strumpet! weep'st thou for him to my face?

(Seizes her by the throat.)

Yet I'll not shed your blood;
Nor scar that whiter skin of yours than snow.

DESDEMONA. O, banish me, my lord, but kill me not!

OTHELLO. Down, strumpet!

DESDEMONA. Kill me to-morrow: let me live to-night!

OTHELLO. Nay, if you strive—

DESDEMONA. But half an hour!

OTHELLO. Being done, there is no pause.

DESDEMONA. But while I say one prayer!

OTHELLO. It is too late.

(He stifles her.)

OPHELIA. Help! help, ho! help! O lady, speak again!
Sweet Desdemona! O sweet mistress, speak!

DESDEMONA. O, falsely, falsely murder'd!

OTHELLO. What noise is this? Not dead? not yet quite dead?
Yet she must die, else she'll betray more men.

(**OTHELLO** *pulls* **OPHELIA** *away and strangles* **DESDEMONA** *again.*)

I that am cruel am yet merciful;
I would not have thee linger in thy pain: So, so.

(**DESDEMONA** *dies.*)

OPHELIA. The Moor hath kill'd my mistress! Murder! murder!

OTHELLO. She is a liar, gone to burning hell.

OPHELIA. Why, how now, ho! from whence ariseth this?
Why should you call her whore? who keeps her company?
What place? what time? what form? what likelihood?

OTHELLO. I know this act shows horrible and grim.
O, I were damn'd beneath all depth in hell,
But that I did proceed upon just grounds
To this extremity. Thy father knew it all.

OPHELIA. My father!

OTHELLO. Thy father.

OPHELIA. That she was false to wedlock?

OTHELLO. Ay, 'twas he that told me first:
'Tis pitiful; but yet Iago knew
That she with Hamlet hath the act of shame
A thousand times committed; Hamlet did top her.

OPHELIA. She false with Hamlet!—did you say with Hamlet?

OTHELLO. With Hamlet, mistress. Go to, charm your tongue.
And she did gratify his amorous works
With that recognizance and pledge of love
Which I first gave her; I saw it in his hand:
It was a handkerchief, an antique token
My father gave my mother.

OPHELIA. O thou dull Moor! that handkerchief thou speak'st of
I found by fortune and did give my father;

    For often, with a solemn earnestness,
    He begg'd of me to steal it.
OTHELLO.   Villainous whore!
OPHELIA. She give it Hamlet! no, alas! I found it,
    And I did give't my father.
IAGO.   Filth, thou liest!
OPHELIA. By heaven, I do not, I do not, gentlemen.
    Poor Desdemona! I am glad my father's dead:
    He told a lie, an odious, damnèd lie;
    Upon my soul, a lie, a wicked lie.
OTHELLO. What? is that true?

    *(Seizes **HAMLET**.)*

                               Confess yourself to heaven;
    Take heed of perjury; thou art on thy deathbed.
    How came you, Hamlet, by that handkerchief
    That was my wife's?
HAMLET.   I found it in my chamber:
    That there he dropp'd it for a special purpose
    Which wrought to his desire.
OTHELLO.   O fool! fool! fool!
OPHELIA. O murderous coxcomb! what should such a fool
    Do with so good a woman?
OTHELLO.   O! O! O!
OPHELIA. Villain, thou diest!

    (**OPHELIA** *lunges at* **OTHELLO***; Again, he easily defends himself against a weakened opponent, but she knocks him to the ground.*)

ALL. Help, ho! murder! murder!
OTHELLO. O, yet defend me, friends; I am but hurt.

    (**HAMLET** *falls upon him, too, and forces the poisoned drink down his throat.*)

HAMLET. Here, thou remorseless, murderous, damnèd Moor,

Drink off this potion. Is thy union here?
Follow my mother.

OPHELIA. He is justly served;
It is a poison temper'd by himself.
Exchange forgiveness with me, noble Hamlet:
Mine and my father's death come not upon thee,
Nor thine on me.

HAMLET. Amen to that, sweet powers!
I cannot speak enough of this content;

(Kissing her.)

And this, and this, the greatest discords be
That e'er our hearts shall make!

OPHELIA. What did thy song bode, lady?
Hark, canst thou hear me? I will play the swan.
And die in music.

[Singing] Willow, willow, willow,—

Moor, she was chaste; she loved thee, cruel Moor;
So come my soul to bliss, as I speak true;
So speaking as I think, I die, I die.

(Dies.)

OTHELLO. O insupportable! O heavy hour!
O Desdemona! Desdemona! dead!
Now, how dost thou look now? O ill-starr'd wench!
Pale as thy smock! when we shall meet at compt,
This look of thine will hurl my soul from heaven,
And fiends will snatch at it. Cold, cold, my girl!
Oh, oh, oh.
I kiss'd thee ere I kill'd thee: no way but this;
Killing myself, to die upon a kiss.

(Stabs himself, falls on the bed, and dies.)

MARCELLUS. O bloody period!
HAMLET. I follow thee.
I am dead, Horatio. Wretched queen, adieu!

(Tries to stand.)

HORATIO. I do beseech you, sir, trouble yourself no further.

HAMLET. O, pardon me: 'twill do me good to walk.
My good friends, I'll leave you to-night: you are welcome to Elsinore.
Had I but time—as this fell sergeant, death,
Is strict in his arrest—O, I could tell you—
But let it be. Horatio, I am dead.

HORATIO. Here's yet some liquor left.

HAMLET.   As thou'rt a man,
Give me the cup: let go; by heaven, I'll have't.
O good Horatio, what a wounded name,
Things standing thus unknown, shall live behind me!
If thou didst ever hold me in thy heart
Absent thee from felicity awhile,
And in this harsh world draw thy breath in pain,
To tell my story. O, I die, Horatio;
The potent poison quite o'er-crows my spirit:
The rest is silence.

(Dies.)

HORATIO. Now cracks a noble heart. Good night sweet prince:
And flights of angels sing thee to thy rest!
[Aside] You that look pale and tremble at this chance,
That are but mutes or audience to this act,
When you shall these unlucky deeds relate,
Speak of them as they are; nothing extenuate,
Nor set down aught in malice: then must you tell
Of some that loved not wisely but too well.
Take up the bodies: such a sight as this
Becomes the field, but here shows much amiss.
Myself will straight abroad: and to the state
This heavy act with heavy heart relate.

(Exeunt.)

SOURCES

The sources for this play are William Shakespeare's *The Tragedie of Hamlet, Prince of Denmarke* (1600-1) and *The Tragedie of Othello, the Moore of Venice* (1604).

The author is indebted to the invaluable online resources of MIT's Shakespeare website (http://shakespeare.mit.edu/) and the Complete Moby™ Shakespeare.

NOTES ON THE TEXT

Every effort was made to preserve the rhythm, language and poetry of the original sources, particularly in the verse sections of the play.

A certain amount of rewording is necessary as a practical matter of fusing the two texts. For example, combining the role of Ophelia with Laertes requires that numerous instances of "he" be replaced with "she," and "him" with "her", etc.

Whenever possible, replacement text is matched syllable-for-syllable. Thus, in verse sections, "man" might be replaced with "maid," rather than "woman," to preserve the meter.

Always, the objective is to ensure that the original rhyme scheme, pronunciation and operative words are not inadvertently affected by modifications in the storyline.

Also by
Jeff Goode

The Eight: Reindeer Monologues

The Messy Adventures of Dick Piston, Hotel Detective

Princess Gray and the Black & White Knights

Romeo and Julius [Caesar]

Rumpelstiltskin

Seven Santas

The Ubu Plays

Your Swash Is Unbuckled

Please consult the
Baker's Plays Catalogue
for complete details or find us online at
www.bakersplays.com

www.ingramcontent.com/pod-product-compliance
Lightning Source LLC
Chambersburg PA
CBHW071833290426
44109CB00017B/1813